THIS BOOK BELONGS TO

_____

_____

START DATE _____ / _____ / _____

HE READS TRUTH

FOUNDERS

FOUNDER
Raechel Myers

CO-FOUNDER
Amanda Bible Williams

EXECUTIVE

CHIEF EXECUTIVE OFFICER
Ryan Myers

CHIEF BRAND & MARKETING OFFICER
Amy Dennis

CHIEF CONTENT OFFICER
Jessica Lamb

CHIEF OPERATING OFFICER
Raechel Myers

EDITORIAL

PRODUCTION EDITOR
Hannah Little, MTS

MARKETING CONTENT EDITOR
Tameshia Williams, ThM

ASSOCIATE EDITORS
Kayla De La Torre, MAT
Lindsey Jacobi, MDiv

COPY EDITOR
Becca Owens

MARKETING

SENIOR MARKETING MANAGER
Katie Bevels

MARKETING PROJECT COORDINATOR
Kyndal Kearns

GROWTH MARKETING MANAGER
Blake Showalter

PRODUCT MARKETING MANAGER
Whitney Hoffman

SOCIAL MEDIA STRATEGIST
Taylor Krupp

CREATIVE

DESIGN MANAGER
Kelsea Allen

ART DIRECTORS
Annie Glover
Lauren Haag

DESIGNER
Ashley Phillips

JUNIOR DESIGNER
Jessie Gerakinis

OPERATIONS

OPERATIONS DIRECTOR
Allison Sutton

OPERATIONS COORDINATOR
Mary Beth Steed

SHIPPING

SHIPPING MANAGER
Marian Byne

FULFILLMENT LEAD
Kajsa Matheny

FULFILLMENT SPECIALIST
Hannah Lamb

SUBSCRIPTION INQUIRIES
orders@hereadstruth.com

COMMUNITY SUPPORT

COMMUNITY EXPERIENCE DIRECTOR
Kara Hewett, MOL

COMMUNITY SUPPORT SPECIALISTS
Katy McKnight
Alecia Rohrer
Heather Vollono

CONTRIBUTORS

RECIPE
Christina Stainbrook (83)

SPECIAL THANKS
Abbey Benson
Amanda Brush

COLOPHON

This book was printed offset in Nashville, Tennessee, on 60# Lynx Opaque Text under the direction of He Reads Truth. Cover is 100# Cougar Opaque with a soft touch lamination.

COPYRIGHT

© 2023 by He Reads Truth, LLC
All rights reserved.
All photography used by permission.

ISBN 978-1-952670-92-3

1 2 3 4 5 6 7 8 9 10

No part of this publication may be reproduced, distributed, or transmitted in any form or by any means, including photocopying, recording, or other electronic or mechanical methods, without the prior written permission of He Reads Truth, LLC, except in the case of brief quotations embodied in critical reviews and certain other noncommercial uses Unless ermitted by copyright law.

All Scripture is taken from the Christian Standard Bible®. Copyright © 2020 by Holman Bible Publishers. Used by permission. Christian Standard Bible® and CSB® are federally registered trademarks of Holman Bible Publishers.

"O Come, Let Us Adore Him" score provided by Hymnary.org.

Research support provided by Logos Bible Software™. Learn more at logos.com.

HEREADSTRUTH.COM   @HEREADSTRUTH   Download the He Reads Truth app, available for iOS and Android

ADVENT 2023
HE ALONE IS WORTHY

HE READS TRUTH

THIS IS WHAT THE SEASON OF ADVENT IS ABOUT: ANTICIPATING THE BIRTH OF THE ONE WHO MEETS EVERY NEED.

WELCOME LETTER

Think about your childhood heroes. Do you ever wonder what life was really like for them? It can be easy to consider those we admire from generations past as larger than life figures, immune to the struggles of living in this not-yet-fully-restored world. But, like us, they too experienced longings—for painful relationships to be repaired, for ailing bodies to be healed, for deeply held hopes to become reality, for mounds of uncertainty to be overcome with surety. Like us, they likely found themselves limping toward Christmas Day, an ache for restoration embedded in their hearts.

We've been thinking about that reality as we hold this year's Advent reading plan in our hands, about how each generation is united to those before and after by a bones-deep desire for everything to be made right. We see it throughout the Old Testament as God's people waited for the Messiah. We hear its echo in the New Testament as the early Church waited for Christ's return. We recognize it in the words of the O Antiphon prayers as believers in the Middle Ages voiced their longing for and trust in Jesus. And we feel it still today as we remember the birth of our Savior and look forward to His promised return.

This is what the season of Advent is about: anticipating the birth of the One who meets every need. Jesus is the man from heaven who came to reconcile us to God. He is the bread of life who satisfies our deepest hunger. He is the King of the nations who brings the hope of heaven to the whole world. He is God with us, the only one worthy of our worship.

We are thrilled that you're joining us for this Advent season. Together we will celebrate the season with food and song. We will reflect and anticipate. We will read the ancient prophecies of the Savior and rejoice in their fulfillment. And we will look with hope to the promised day when every nation and generation will know full and lasting peace in the presence of Jesus.

O come, let us adore Him! For He alone is worthy—Christ the Lord.

THE HE READS TRUTH TEAM

DESIGN ON PURPOSE

Each He Reads Truth resource is thoughtfully and artfully designed to highlight the beauty, goodness, and truth of Scripture in a way that reflects the themes of each curated reading plan.

For this book, we drew inspiration from our memories of Christmases past and the excitement of anticipating traditions of the holiday season. We staged and photographed the scenes featured throughout the book to create a sense of joy, warmth, and nostalgia. The photography throughout the book shows scenes of invitation, hope, and home. We paired these photos with a rich, traditional Christmas color palette to evoke the comfort of knowing that Christ has fulfilled our every need. The intricate patterns scattered in the book represent how Christ fulfills the longings woven throughout the Old Testament. Each pattern included in this book has a hand-drawn appearance to reflect how we each experience Christ's hope in our individual lives. Negative space also features prominently in the layouts. This is meant to provide an invitation to contemplation—space to sit, reflect, converse, and acknowledge the needs we have to see where Scripture describes God's fulfillment of each and every one.

When combined, these elements convey a sense of eager expectation as we celebrate and long for God's presence this Advent season.

HOW TO USE THIS BOOK

He Reads Truth is a community of men dedicated to reading the Word of God every day. In this **Advent 2023** reading plan, we will read passages from across the Bible as we explore the biblical anticipation of Jesus and how His arrival meets every expectation and longing.

READ & REFLECT

Your **Advent 2023** book focuses primarily on Scripture, with added features to come alongside your time with God's Word.

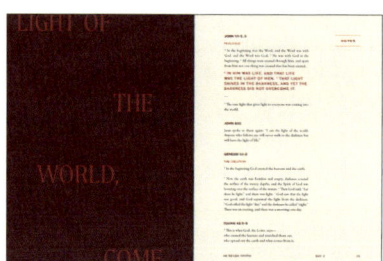

SCRIPTURE READING

Designed for a Sunday start, this book presents daily Scripture readings for the Advent season.

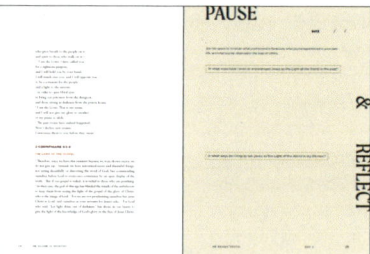

REFLECTION

Throughout this book, you'll find questions for personal reflection and space to respond in prayer.

COMMUNITY & CONVERSATION

You can start reading this book at any time. If you want to join men from across the globe as they read along with you, the He Reads Truth community will start Day 1 of **Advent 2023** on Sunday, December 3, 2023.

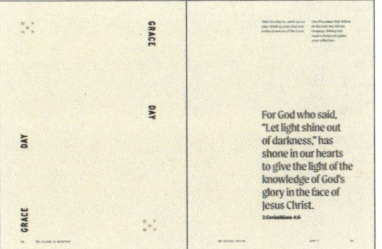

GRACE DAY

Use Saturdays to catch up on your reading, pray, and rest in the presence of the Lord.

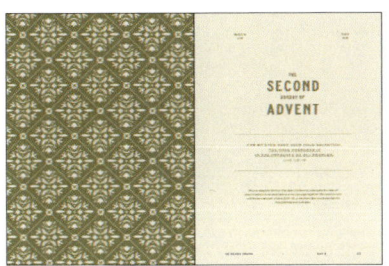

SUNDAYS

The Sundays in Advent are set aside for Scripture memorization and meditation.

See tips for memorizing Scripture on page 164.

EXTRAS

This book features additional tools to help you gain a deeper understanding of the text.

Find a complete list of extras on page 13.

HE READS TRUTH APP

Devotionals corresponding to each daily reading can be found in the **Advent 2023** reading plan on the He Reads Truth app. Devotionals will be published each weekday once the plan begins on Sunday, December 3, 2023. You can use the app to participate in community discussion and more.

HEREADSTRUTH.COM

The **Advent 2023** reading plan and devotionals will also be available at HeReadsTruth.com as the community reads each day. Invite your family, friends, and neighbors to read along with you.

TABLE OF CONTENTS

WEEK

01

DAY 1	The First Sunday of Advent	21
DAY 2	Light of the World, Come	22
DAY 3	Man from Heaven, Come	37
DAY 4	Blessing for All People, Come	42
DAY 5	Generous Provider, Come	50
DAY 6	Perfect Sacrifice, Come	54
DAY 7	Grace Day	58

Week 1 Response — 60

WEEK

02

DAY 8	The Second Sunday of Advent	63
DAY 9	Bread of Life, Come	64
DAY 10	Living Water, Come	69
DAY 11	Restorer of Life, Come	74
DAY 12	Righteous Mediator, Come	78
DAY 13	Great High Priest, Come	84
DAY 14	Grace Day	88

Week 2 Response — 90

WEEK

03

DAY 15	The Third Sunday of Advent	93
DAY 16	Lord, Come	94
DAY 17	Root of Jesse, Come	98
DAY 18	Key of David, Come	102
DAY 19	Morning Star, Come	109
DAY 20	King of the Nations, Come	114
DAY 21	Grace Day	120

WEEK

04

DAY 22	Christmas Eve: Immanuel Has Come	122
DAY 23	Christmas Day: The Savior of the World Has Come	131
DAY 24	The Glorious One Has Come	136
DAY 25	The Eternal King Has Come	142
DAY 26	The Holy Spirit Has Come	146
DAY 27	The Everlasting One Will Come Again	152
DAY 28	Grace Day	156
DAY 29	The Last Sunday of the Year	159

EXTRAS

Introduction to Advent	14
Practicing the Presence of God in Advent	26
Christmas and the Seasons of the Church	106
Christmas Day Reflection	135
For the Record	160

HYMNS

Ding Dong! Merrily on High	48
Angels, from the Realms of Glory	128
Joy to the World! The Lord Is Come	140
O Come, Let Us Adore Him	150

RECIPE

All-Day Spiced Cider	83

INTRODUCTION TO ADVENT

KEY ── PASSAGE

For my eyes have seen your salvation. You have prepared it in the presence of all peoples.

Luke 2:30–31

(WHAT IS ADVENT?)

Advent is a Latin word that means "coming" or "arrival." On the Church calendar, the season of Advent begins four Sundays before Christmas Day and culminates on Christmas Eve. It is a season full of hope, expectation, and longing.

Since the fourth century, Christians have observed Advent as a time to remember both Jesus's first advent (His coming as a baby born in Bethlehem) and anticipate His second advent (His triumphant future return).

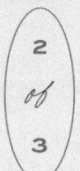

ADVENT 2023

The O Antiphon prayers will guide us in our 2023 Advent journey, reminding us how Jesus alone meets our deepest needs.

The **O Antiphons**, seven prayers based on biblical prophecies about Jesus, have been part of Advent worship in the Church since the Middle Ages. Traditionally, one antiphon is sung or prayed each night of the week leading up to Christmas Eve, from December 17 through December 23. Each prayer begins by addressing Jesus with one of the titles used for Him in Scripture, and is followed by a plea for Him to "come" in specific capacities.

This reading plan explores many of the unique ways Jesus fulfilled every hope, expectation, and longing of people of the Old Testament. For the week leading to Christmas, our readings will focus specifically on the longings present in the seven O Antiphon prayers, and we will pray one on each day of the week leading up to Christmas.

Then, in the final week of this reading plan, we will celebrate the way Jesus continues to meet our needs as we wait for the day He will come again.

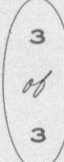

When read in reverse, the first letters of these Latin titles spell *ero cras*, which means, "Tomorrow, I will come."

E R O

O EMMANUEL
DECEMBER 23

O REX GENTIUM
DECEMBER 22

O ORIENS
DECEMBER 21

O Emmanuel, our king and our lawgiver, the hope of the nations and their Saviour: Come and save us, O Lord our God.

O King of the nations, and their desire, the cornerstone making both one: Come and save the human race, which you fashioned from clay.

O Morning Star, splendour of light eternal and sun of righteousness: Come and enlighten those who dwell in darkness and the shadow of death.

C R A S

O CLAVIS DAVID	**O RADIX JESSE**	**O ADONAI**	**O SAPIENTIA**
DECEMBER 20	DECEMBER 19	DECEMBER 18	DECEMBER 17

O Key of David, and sceptre of the House of Israel; you open and no one can shut; you shut and no one can open: Come and lead the prisoners from the prison house, those who dwell in darkness and the shadow of death.

O Root of Jesse, standing as a sign among the peoples; before you kings will shut their mouths, to you the nations will make their prayer: Come and deliver us, and delay no longer.

O Lord, and leader of the House of Israel, who appeared to Moses in the fire of the burning bush and gave him the law on Sinai: Come and redeem us with an outstretched arm.

O Wisdom, coming forth from the mouth of the Most High, reaching from one end to the other, mightily and sweetly ordering all things: Come and teach us the way of prudence.

WEEK 01

DAY 01

THE
FIRST
SUNDAY OF
ADVENT

FOR MY EYES HAVE SEEN YOUR SALVATION.
YOU HAVE PREPARED IT
IN THE PRESENCE OF ALL PEOPLES.
LUKE 2:30–31

Advent is a season where we remember why the Son of God came to dwell with us on earth, and the hope that He is coming again. Yet, this time on the calendar can quickly fill with distractions and to-dos, or even heaviness and grief. Even still, the reality that God has come to us in our humanity means we can bring all our messiness and weariness to Him as we engage in this spiritually rich season. We invite you to use the first two Sundays of Advent to store up in your heart the hope of Jesus's arrival to encourage you in the days to come.

For the next two weeks, we will spend time memorizing our key passage. This week we will memorize the first part of Luke 2:30–31.

LIGHT OF

DAY TWO

THE

WORLD,

COME

JOHN 1:1-5, 9

PROLOGUE

¹ In the beginning was the Word, and the Word was with God, and the Word was God. ² He was with God in the beginning. ³ All things were created through him, and apart from him not one thing was created that has been created.

⁴ **IN HIM WAS LIFE, AND THAT LIFE WAS THE LIGHT OF MEN. ⁵ THAT LIGHT SHINES IN THE DARKNESS, AND YET THE DARKNESS DID NOT OVERCOME IT.**

…

⁹ The true light that gives light to everyone was coming into the world.

JOHN 8:12

Jesus spoke to them again: "I am the light of the world. Anyone who follows me will never walk in the darkness but will have the light of life."

GENESIS 1:1-5

THE CREATION

¹ In the beginning God created the heavens and the earth.

² Now the earth was formless and empty, darkness covered the surface of the watery depths, and the Spirit of God was hovering over the surface of the waters. ³ Then God said, "Let there be light," and there was light. ⁴ God saw that the light was good, and God separated the light from the darkness. ⁵ God called the light "day," and the darkness he called "night." There was an evening, and there was a morning: one day.

ISAIAH 42:5-9

⁵ This is what God, the Lord, says—
who created the heavens and stretched them out,
who spread out the earth and what comes from it,

NOTES

who gives breath to the people on it
and spirit to those who walk on it—
6 "I am the LORD. I have called you
for a righteous purpose,
and I will hold you by your hand.
I will watch over you, and I will appoint you
to be a covenant for the people
and a light to the nations,
7 in order to open blind eyes,
to bring out prisoners from the dungeon,
and those sitting in darkness from the prison house.
8 I am the LORD. That is my name,
and I will not give my glory to another
or my praise to idols.
9 The past events have indeed happened.
Now I declare new events;
I announce them to you before they occur."

2 CORINTHIANS 4:1–6

THE LIGHT OF THE GOSPEL

1 Therefore, since we have this ministry because we were shown mercy, we
do not give up. 2 Instead, we have renounced secret and shameful things,
not acting deceitfully or distorting the word of God, but commending
ourselves before God to everyone's conscience by an open display of the
truth. 3 But if our gospel is veiled, it is veiled to those who are perishing.
4 In their case, the god of this age has blinded the minds of the unbelievers
to keep them from seeing the light of the gospel of the glory of Christ,
who is the image of God. 5 For we are not proclaiming ourselves but Jesus
Christ as Lord, and ourselves as your servants for Jesus's sake. 6 For God
who said, "Let light shine out of darkness," has shone in our hearts to
give the light of the knowledge of God's glory in the face of Jesus Christ.

PAUSE

DATE / /

Use this space to consider what you've read in Scripture, what you've experienced in your own life, and what you've observed in the lives of others.

In what ways have I seen or experienced Jesus as the Light of the World in the past?

In what ways do I long to see Jesus as the Light of the World in my life now?

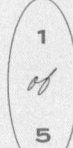

PRACTICING THE PRESENCE OF GOD IN ADVENT

During Advent, we intentionally practice slowing down our rhythms, taking time to remember why the Son of God came to dwell with us on earth and the hope that He is coming again. In this in-between period, we remember God's promise to never leave us. The Holy Spirit is present with every believer, and Jesus told us He would be with us always (Mt 28:20; Jn 14:16–17). Throughout this season, make time to practice the presence of God using the tips and reminders on the following pages as a guide.

MAKE INTENTIONAL TIME AND SPACE

Though we often experience the presence of God with other believers at church or other gatherings, we also need to spend time alone with Him. When we create space and margin for Him in our lives, we may be surprised by how He fills it with His presence.

PRAY

In Scripture, prayer takes on many forms and postures in conversation with God (Ps 5:7; Dn 6:10; Mt 26:39). These practices are not a means of making God more able to hear from us. Instead, prayer is a way of focusing our hearts and minds on God's presence as we navigate everyday life.

MEDITATE ON GOD'S WORD

Meditating on God's Word means taking time to slowly read and think about Scripture and what it tells us about who God is.

WORSHIP

Embrace God's presence through worship.

MAKE INTENTIONAL TIME AND SPACE

CHOOSE A TIME

Consider how you can devote parts of your current daily rhythm to connect with God. Start by choosing a time in advance and blocking it on your calendar. Carve out fifteen minutes in the morning or before you go to bed, or find a quiet spot during your lunch break.

DECIDE ON A PLACE

Decide on a place—in your home, by your Christmas tree, in your car, or even outside with a warm blanket.

MINIMIZE DISTRACTIONS

Minimize distractions. Turn off your television, phone, and other devices.

MEDITATE ON GOD'S WORD

PAUSE

As you read through your daily Scripture reading, pause to slowly take the words in.

REREAD

Reread verses that stand out to you, saying them out loud or writing them down to focus on specific parts of the reading.

MEMORIZE

Memorize individual verses or longer passages to help you internalize or summarize a larger theme in what you have read. Consider memorizing the key passage on page 15 as a reminder of God's salvation and faithfulness toward His people.

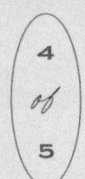

PRAY

BEGIN

Begin your reading with prayer. Ask God to meet with you, speak to you, and help you reflect on Christ's coming in a fresh way.

USE THE O ANTIPHONS

Incorporate the O Antiphon prayers into your routines this season. Consider repeating them as you get ready, before you eat, or as you are preparing your meals.

CONSIDER OTHERS

Pray for your family and friends as you wrap gifts, fill stockings, or drive to gatherings. Ask specifically that God would remind them during this season how Christ meets their deepest needs.

LISTEN

Spend time not only talking to God, but listening as well. Intentionally pause from your work at home or in the office. Depending on your normal posture, pair your prayer with either movement or stillness. Actively listen in a quiet, unhurried way. Practice focusing your thoughts on God instead of your tasks and to-do lists.

WORSHIP

LISTEN

Spend time listening to your favorite Christmas playlist as you prepare for holiday activities—like running errands, cleaning, cooking, or decorating.

PARTICIPATE

Turn to the Christmas sheet music on pages 48, 128, 140, and 150. Dance, sing, or play a musical instrument along with the lyrics chosen for this year's reading plan.

ENGAGE WITH OTHERS

Engage in corporate worship with your local church through a Christmas Eve or special holiday service.

SERVE

As you prepare to give donations or gifts, consider how your time, money, and presence can be an act of service to those around you. Look for ways you can act as the hands and feet of Christ toward your friends, family, community, and your local church.

MAN FROM HEAVEN, COME

WEEK 01

DAY 03

GENESIS 2:15-17

[15] The Lord God took the man and placed him in the garden of Eden to work it and watch over it. [16] And the Lord God commanded the man, "You are free to eat from any tree of the garden, [17] but you must not eat from the tree of the knowledge of good and evil, for on the day you eat from it, you will certainly die."

GENESIS 3:1-13, 17-19, 22-24

THE TEMPTATION AND THE FALL

[1] Now the serpent was the most cunning of all the wild animals that the Lord God had made. He said to the woman, "Did God really say, 'You can't eat from any tree in the garden'?"

[2] The woman said to the serpent, "We may eat the fruit from the trees in the garden. [3] But about the fruit of the tree in the middle of the garden, God said, 'You must not eat it or touch it, or you will die.'"

[4] "No! You will certainly not die," the serpent said to the woman. [5] "In fact, God knows that when you eat it your eyes will be opened and you will be like God, knowing good and evil." [6] The woman saw that the tree was good for food and delightful to look at, and that it was desirable for obtaining wisdom. So she took some of its fruit and ate it; she also gave some to her husband, who was with her, and he ate it. [7] Then the eyes of both of them were opened, and they knew they were naked; so they sewed fig leaves together and made coverings for themselves.

SIN'S CONSEQUENCES

[8] Then the man and his wife heard the sound of the Lord God walking in the garden at the time of the evening breeze, and they hid from the Lord God among the trees of the garden. [9] So the Lord God called out to the man and said to him, "Where are you?"

[10] And he said, "I heard you in the garden, and I was afraid because I was naked, so I hid."

[11] Then he asked, "Who told you that you were naked? Did you eat from the tree that I commanded you not to eat from?"

¹² The man replied, "The woman you gave to be with me—she gave me some fruit from the tree, and I ate."

¹³ So the LORD God asked the woman, "What have you done?"

And the woman said, "The serpent deceived me, and I ate."

...

¹⁷ And he said to the man, "Because you listened to your wife and ate from the tree about which I commanded you, 'Do not eat from it':

> The ground is cursed because of you.
> You will eat from it by means of painful labor
> all the days of your life.
> ¹⁸ It will produce thorns and thistles for you,
> and you will eat the plants of the field.
> ¹⁹ You will eat bread by the sweat of your brow
> until you return to the ground,
> since you were taken from it.
> For you are dust,
> and you will return to dust."

...

²² The LORD God said, "Since the man has become like one of us, knowing good and evil, he must not reach out, take from the tree of life, eat, and live forever." ²³ So the LORD God sent him away from the garden of Eden to work the ground from which he was taken. ²⁴ He drove the man out and stationed the cherubim and the flaming, whirling sword east of the garden of Eden to guard the way to the tree of life.

ROMANS 5:12–21

DEATH THROUGH ADAM AND LIFE THROUGH CHRIST

¹² Therefore, just as sin entered the world through one man, and death through sin, in this way death spread to all people, because all sinned. ¹³ In fact, sin was in the world before the law, but sin is not charged to a person's account when there is no law. ¹⁴ Nevertheless, death reigned from Adam to Moses, even over those who did not sin in the likeness of Adam's transgression. He is a type of the Coming One.

¹⁵ But the gift is not like the trespass. For if by the one man's trespass the many died, how much more have the grace of God and the gift which comes through the grace of the one man Jesus Christ overflowed to the many. ¹⁶ And the gift is not like the one man's sin, because from one sin came the judgment, resulting in condemnation, but from many trespasses came the gift, resulting in justification. ¹⁷ If by the one man's trespass, death reigned through that one man, how much more will those who receive the overflow of grace and the gift of righteousness reign in life through the one man, Jesus Christ.

¹⁸ So then, as through one trespass there is condemnation for everyone, so also through one righteous act there is justification leading to life for everyone. ¹⁹ For just as through one man's disobedience the many were made sinners, so also through the one man's obedience the many will be made righteous. ²⁰ The law came along to multiply the trespass. But where sin multiplied, grace multiplied even more ²¹ so that, just as sin reigned in death, so also grace will reign through righteousness, resulting in eternal life through Jesus Christ our Lord.

1 CORINTHIANS 15:20–22, 47–49

CHRIST'S RESURRECTION GUARANTEES OURS

²⁰ But as it is, Christ has been raised from the dead, the firstfruits of those who have fallen asleep. ²¹ For since death came through a man, the resurrection of the dead also comes through a man.

²² FOR JUST AS IN ADAM ALL DIE, SO ALSO IN CHRIST ALL WILL BE MADE ALIVE.

...

⁴⁷ The first man was from the earth, a man of dust; the second man is from heaven. ⁴⁸ Like the man of dust, so are those who are of the dust; like the man of heaven, so are those who are of heaven. ⁴⁹ And just as we have borne the image of the man of dust, we will also bear the image of the man of heaven.

PAUSE

DATE / /

In what ways have I seen or experienced Jesus as the man from heaven in the past?

In what ways do I long to see Jesus as the man from heaven in my life now?

BLESSING FOR ALL PEOPLE, COME

DAY 04

ALL THE NATIONS WILL BE
BLESSED THROUGH YOU

GALATIANS 3:8

GENESIS 15:1-6

THE ABRAHAMIC COVENANT

¹ After these events, the word of the Lord came to Abram in a vision:

> Do not be afraid, Abram.
> I am your shield;

your reward will be very great.

² But Abram said, "Lord God, what can you give me, since I am childless and the heir of my house is Eliezer of Damascus?" ³ Abram continued, "Look, you have given me no offspring, so a slave born in my house will be my heir."

⁴ Now the word of the Lord came to him: "This one will not be your heir; instead, one who comes from your own body will be your heir." ⁵ He took him outside and said, "Look at the sky and count the stars, if you are able to count them." Then he said to him, "Your offspring will be that numerous."

⁶ Abram believed the Lord, and he credited it to him as righteousness.

GENESIS 17:1-8, 15-21

¹ When Abram was ninety-nine years old, the Lord appeared to him, saying, "I am God Almighty. Live in my presence and be blameless. ² I will set up my covenant between me and you, and I will multiply you greatly."

³ Then Abram fell facedown and God spoke with him: ⁴ "As for me, here is my covenant with you: You will become the father of many nations. ⁵ Your name will no longer be Abram; your name will be Abraham, for I will make you the father of many nations. ⁶ I will make you extremely fruitful and will make nations and kings come from you. ⁷ I will confirm my covenant that is between me and you and your future offspring throughout their generations. It is a permanent covenant to be your God and the God of your offspring after you. ⁸ And to you and your future offspring I will give the land where you are residing—all the land of Canaan—as a permanent possession, and I will be their God."

...

NOTES

NOTES

¹⁵ God said to Abraham, "As for your wife Sarai, do not call her Sarai, for Sarah will be her name. ¹⁶ I will bless her; indeed, I will give you a son by her. I will bless her, and she will produce nations; kings of peoples will come from her."

¹⁷ Abraham fell facedown. Then he laughed and said to himself, "Can a child be born to a hundred-year-old man? Can Sarah, a ninety-year-old woman, give birth?" ¹⁸ So Abraham said to God, "If only Ishmael were acceptable to you!"

¹⁹ But God said, "No. Your wife Sarah will bear you a son, and you will name him Isaac. I will confirm my covenant with him as a permanent covenant for his future offspring. ²⁰ As for Ishmael, I have heard you. I will certainly bless him; I will make him fruitful and will multiply him greatly. He will father twelve tribal leaders, and I will make him into a great nation. ²¹ But I will confirm my covenant with Isaac, whom Sarah will bear to you at this time next year."

JOHN 8:31–59

³¹ Then Jesus said to the Jews who had believed him, "If you continue in my word, you really are my disciples. ³² You will know the truth, and the truth will set you free."

³³ "We are descendants of Abraham," they answered him, "and we have never been enslaved to anyone. How can you say, 'You will become free'?"

³⁴ Jesus responded, "Truly I tell you, everyone who commits sin is a slave of sin. ³⁵ A slave does not remain in the household forever, but a son does remain forever. ³⁶ So if the Son sets you free, you really will be free. ³⁷ I know you are descendants of Abraham, but you are trying to kill me because my word has no place among you. ³⁸ I speak what I have seen in the presence of the Father; so then, you do what you have heard from your father."

³⁹ "Our father is Abraham," they replied.

"If you were Abraham's children," Jesus told them, "you would do what Abraham did. ⁴⁰ But now you are trying to kill me, a man who has told you the truth that I heard from God. Abraham did not do this. ⁴¹ You're doing what your father does."

"We weren't born of sexual immorality," they said. "We have one Father—God."

⁴² Jesus said to them, "If God were your Father, you would love me, because I came from God and I am here. For I didn't come on my own, but he sent me. ⁴³ Why don't you understand what I say? Because you cannot listen to my word. ⁴⁴ You are of your father the devil, and you want to carry out your father's desires. He was a murderer from the beginning and does not stand in the truth, because there is no truth in him. When he tells a lie, he speaks from his own nature, because he is a liar and the father of lies. ⁴⁵ Yet because I tell the truth, you do not believe me. ⁴⁶ Who among you can convict me of sin? If I am telling the truth, why don't you believe me? ⁴⁷ The one who is from God listens to God's words. This is why you don't listen, because you are not from God."

JESUS AND ABRAHAM

⁴⁸ The Jews responded to him, "Aren't we right in saying that you're a Samaritan and have a demon?"

⁴⁹ "I do not have a demon," Jesus answered. "On the contrary, I honor my Father and you dishonor me. ⁵⁰ I do not seek my own glory; there is one who seeks it and judges. ⁵¹ Truly I tell you, if anyone keeps my word, he will never see death."

⁵² Then the Jews said, "Now we know you have a demon. Abraham died and so did the prophets. You say, 'If anyone keeps my word, he will never taste death.' ⁵³ Are you greater than our father Abraham who died? And the prophets died. Who do you claim to be?"

⁵⁴ "If I glorify myself," Jesus answered, "my glory is nothing. My Father—about whom you say, 'He is our God'—he is the one who glorifies me. ⁵⁵ You do not know him, but I know him. If I were to say I don't know him, I would be a liar like you. But I do know him, and I keep his word. ⁵⁶ Your father Abraham rejoiced to see my day; he saw it and was glad."

NOTES

⁵⁷ The Jews replied, "You aren't fifty years old yet, and you've seen Abraham?"

⁵⁸ Jesus said to them, "Truly I tell you, before Abraham was, I am."

⁵⁹ So they picked up stones to throw at him. But Jesus was hidden and went out of the temple.

GALATIANS 3:7-9, 14-16, 27-29

⁷ You know, then, that those who have faith, these are Abraham's sons. ⁸ Now the Scripture saw in advance that God would justify the Gentiles by faith and proclaimed the gospel ahead of time to Abraham, saying, All the nations will be blessed through you. ⁹ Consequently, those who have faith are blessed with Abraham, who had faith.

...

¹⁴ The purpose was that the blessing of Abraham would come to the Gentiles by Christ Jesus, so that we could receive the promised Spirit through faith.

¹⁵ Brothers and sisters, I'm using a human illustration. No one sets aside or makes additions to a validated human will. ¹⁶ Now the promises were spoken to Abraham and to his seed. He does not say "and to seeds," as though referring to many, but referring to one, and to your seed, who is Christ.

...

SONS AND HEIRS

²⁷ For those of you who were baptized into Christ have been clothed with Christ. ²⁸ There is no Jew or Greek, slave or free, male and female; since you are all one in Christ Jesus. ²⁹ And if you belong to Christ, then you are Abraham's seed, heirs according to the promise.

PAUSE

DATE / /

In what ways have I seen or experienced Jesus as the blessing for all people in the past?

In what ways do I long to see Jesus as the blessing for all people in my life now?

DING DONG!
MERRILY ON HIGH

WORDS: *George Ratcliffe Woodward*   MUSIC: *Charles Wood*

GENESIS 22:1-18

THE SACRIFICE OF ISAAC

¹ After these things God tested Abraham and said to him, "Abraham!"

"Here I am," he answered.

² "Take your son," he said, "your only son Isaac, whom you love, go to the land of Moriah, and offer him there as a burnt offering on one of the mountains I will tell you about."

³ So Abraham got up early in the morning, saddled his donkey, and took with him two of his young men and his son Isaac. He split wood for a burnt offering and set out to go to the place God had told him about. ⁴ On the third day Abraham looked up and saw the place in the distance. ⁵ Then Abraham said to his young men, "Stay here with the donkey. The boy and I will go over there to worship; then we'll come back to you." ⁶ Abraham took the wood for the burnt offering and laid it on his son Isaac. In his hand he took the fire and the knife, and the two of them walked on together.

⁷ Then Isaac spoke to his father Abraham and said, "My father."

And he replied, "Here I am, my son."

Isaac said, "The fire and the wood are here, but where is the lamb for the burnt offering?"

⁸ Abraham answered, "God himself will provide the lamb for the burnt offering, my son." Then the two of them walked on together.

⁹ When they arrived at the place that God had told him about, Abraham built the altar there and arranged the wood. He bound his son Isaac and placed him on the altar on top of the wood. ¹⁰ Then Abraham reached out and took the knife to slaughter his son.

NOTES

¹¹ But the angel of the LORD called to him from heaven and said, "Abraham, Abraham!"

He replied, "Here I am."

¹² Then he said, "Do not lay a hand on the boy or do anything to him. For now I know that you fear God, since you have not withheld your only son from me." ¹³ Abraham looked up and saw a ram caught in the thicket by its horns. So Abraham went and took the ram and offered it as a burnt offering in place of his son. ¹⁴ And Abraham named that place The LORD Will Provide, so today it is said, "It will be provided on the LORD's mountain."

¹⁵ Then the angel of the LORD called to Abraham a second time from heaven ¹⁶ and said, "By myself I have sworn," this is the LORD's declaration:

"BECAUSE YOU HAVE DONE THIS THING AND HAVE NOT WITHHELD YOUR ONLY SON,

¹⁷ I will indeed bless you and make your offspring as numerous as the stars of the sky and the sand on the seashore. Your offspring will possess the city gates of their enemies. ¹⁸ And all the nations of the earth will be blessed by your offspring because you have obeyed my command."

MATTHEW 26:36-46

THE PRAYER IN THE GARDEN

³⁶ Then Jesus came with them to a place called Gethsemane, and he told the disciples, "Sit here while I go over there and pray." ³⁷ Taking along Peter and the two sons of Zebedee, he began to be sorrowful and troubled. ³⁸ He said to them, "I am deeply grieved to the point of death. Remain here and stay awake with me." ³⁹ Going a little farther, he fell facedown and prayed, "My Father, if it is possible, let this cup pass from me. Yet not as I will, but as you will."

⁴⁰ Then he came to the disciples and found them sleeping. He asked Peter, "So, couldn't you stay awake with me one hour? ⁴¹ Stay awake and pray, so that you won't enter into temptation. The spirit is willing, but the flesh is weak."

⁴² Again, a second time, he went away and prayed, "My Father, if this cannot pass unless I drink it, your will be done." ⁴³ And he came again and found them sleeping, because they could not keep their eyes open.

⁴⁴ After leaving them, he went away again and prayed a third time, saying the same thing once more. ⁴⁵ Then he came to the disciples and said to them, "Are you still sleeping and resting? See, the time is near. The Son of Man is betrayed into the hands of sinners. ⁴⁶ Get up; let's go. See, my betrayer is near."

JOHN 3:16

"For God loved the world in this way: He gave his one and only Son, so that everyone who believes in him will not perish but have eternal life."

ROMANS 8:32

He did not even spare his own Son but gave him up for us all. How will he not also with him grant us everything?

PAUSE

DATE / /

In what ways have I seen or experienced Jesus as the generous provider in the past?

In what ways do I long to see Jesus as the generous provider in my life now?

DAY 06

PERFECT SACRIFICE, COME

LEVITICUS 4:32-35

³² "Or if the offering that he brings as a sin offering is a lamb, he is to bring an unblemished female. ³³ He is to lay his hand on the head of the sin offering and slaughter it as a sin offering at the place where the burnt offering is slaughtered. ³⁴ Then the priest is to take some of the blood of the sin offering with his finger and apply it to the horns of the altar of burnt offering. He is to pour out the rest of its blood at the base of the altar. ³⁵ He is to remove all its fat just as the fat of the lamb is removed from the fellowship sacrifice. The priest will burn it on the altar along with the food offerings to the Lord. In this way the priest will make atonement on his behalf for the sin he has committed, and he will be forgiven."

LEVITICUS 16:1-22

THE DAY OF ATONEMENT

¹ The Lord spoke to Moses after the death of two of Aaron's sons when they approached the presence of the Lord and died. ² The Lord said to Moses, "Tell your brother Aaron that he may not come whenever he wants into the holy place behind the curtain in front of the mercy seat on the ark or else he will die, because I appear in the cloud above the mercy seat.

³ "Aaron is to enter the most holy place in this way: with a young bull for a sin offering and a ram for a burnt offering. ⁴ He is to wear a holy linen tunic, and linen undergarments are to be on his body. He is to tie a linen sash around him and wrap his head with a linen turban. These are holy garments; he must bathe his body with water before he wears them. ⁵ He is to take from the Israelite community two male goats for a sin offering and one ram for a burnt offering.

⁶ "Aaron will present the bull for his sin offering and make atonement for himself and his household. ⁷ Next he will take the two goats and place them before the Lord at the entrance to the tent of meeting. ⁸ After Aaron casts lots for the two goats, one lot for the Lord and the other for an uninhabitable place, ⁹ he is to

present the goat chosen by lot for the Lord and sacrifice it as a sin offering. ¹⁰ But the goat chosen by lot for an uninhabitable place is to be presented alive before the Lord to make atonement with it by sending it into the wilderness for an uninhabitable place.

¹¹ "When Aaron presents the bull for his sin offering and makes atonement for himself and his household, he will slaughter the bull for his sin offering. ¹² Then he is to take a firepan full of blazing coals from the altar before the Lord and two handfuls of finely ground fragrant incense, and bring them inside the curtain. ¹³ He is to put the incense on the fire before the Lord, so that the cloud of incense covers the mercy seat that is over the testimony, or else he will die. ¹⁴ He is to take some of the bull's blood and sprinkle it with his finger against the east side of the mercy seat; then he will sprinkle some of the blood with his finger before the mercy seat seven times.

¹⁵ "When he slaughters the male goat for the people's sin offering and brings its blood inside the curtain, he will do the same with its blood as he did with the bull's blood: He is to sprinkle it against the mercy seat and in front of it. ¹⁶ He will make atonement for the most holy place in this way for all their sins because of the Israelites' impurities and rebellious acts. He will do the same for the tent of meeting that remains among them, because it is surrounded by their impurities. ¹⁷ No one may be in the tent of meeting from the time he enters to make atonement in the most holy place until he leaves after he has made atonement for himself, his household, and the whole assembly of Israel. ¹⁸ Then he will go out to the altar that is before the Lord and make atonement for it. He is to take some of the bull's blood and some of the goat's blood and put it on the horns on all sides of the altar. ¹⁹ He is to sprinkle some of the blood on it with his finger seven times to cleanse and set it apart from the Israelites' impurities.

²⁰ "When he has finished making atonement for the most holy place, the tent of meeting, and the altar, he is to present

NOTES

the live male goat. ²¹ Aaron will lay both his hands on the head of the live goat and confess over it all the Israelites' iniquities and rebellious acts—all their sins. He is to put them on the goat's head and send it away into the wilderness by the man appointed for the task. ²² The goat will carry all their iniquities into a desolate land, and the man will release it there."

JOHN 1:29

The next day John saw Jesus coming toward him and said, "Look, the Lamb of God, who takes away the sin of the world!"

HEBREWS 10:1–10

THE PERFECT SACRIFICE

¹ Since the law has only a shadow of the good things to come, and not the reality itself of those things, it can never perfect the worshipers by the same sacrifices they continually offer year after year. ² Otherwise, wouldn't they have stopped being offered, since the worshipers, purified once and for all, would no longer have any consciousness of sins? ³ But in the sacrifices there is a reminder of sins year after year. ⁴ For it is impossible for the blood of bulls and goats to take away sins.

⁵ Therefore, as he was coming into the world, he said:

> You did not desire sacrifice and offering,
> but you prepared a body for me.
> ⁶ You did not delight
> in whole burnt offerings and sin offerings.
> ⁷ Then I said, "See—
> it is written about me
> in the scroll—
> I have come to do your will, God."

⁸ After he says above, You did not desire or delight in sacrifices and offerings, whole burnt offerings and sin offerings (which are offered according to the law), ⁹ he then says, See, I have come to do your will. He takes away the first to establish the second.

¹⁰ BY THIS WILL, WE HAVE BEEN SANCTIFIED THROUGH THE OFFERING OF THE BODY OF JESUS CHRIST ONCE FOR ALL TIME.

2 CORINTHIANS 5:21

He made the one who did not know sin to be sin for us, so that in him we might become the righteousness of God.

1 PETER 1:17–21

¹⁷ If you appeal to the Father who judges impartially according to each one's work, you are to conduct yourselves in reverence during your time living as strangers. ¹⁸ For you know that you were redeemed from your empty way of life inherited from your ancestors, not with perishable things like silver or gold, ¹⁹ but with the precious blood of Christ, like that of an unblemished and spotless lamb. ²⁰ He was foreknown before the foundation of the world but was revealed in these last times for you. ²¹ Through him you believe in God, who raised him from the dead and gave him glory, so that your faith and hope are in God.

PAUSE

DATE   /   /

In what ways have I seen or experienced Jesus as the perfect sacrifice in the past?

In what ways do I long to see Jesus as the perfect sacrifice in my life now?

GRACE DAY

DAY 07

HE ALONE IS WORTHY

Take this day to catch up on your reading, pray, and rest in the presence of the Lord.

Use the pages that follow to express any stirred longings, letting this week's Scripture guide your reflection.

For God who said, "Let light shine out of darkness," has shone in our hearts to give the light of the knowledge of God's glory in the face of Jesus Christ.

2 Corinthians 4:6

RESPONSE

Write a prayer of gratitude, thanking Jesus for who He is.

I praise you, Jesus, for being the _____

_____

_____

_____

_____

_____

_____

_____

_____

_____

_____

_____

_____

_____

_____

_____

WEEK 01

**LIGHT OF THE WORLD | MAN FROM HEAVEN | BLESSING FOR ALL PEOPLE
GENEROUS PROVIDER | PERFECT SACRIFICE**

Write a prayer of longing, expressing your desire
to see this aspect of Jesus in your life.

Come, _____

DATE / /

LIGHT OF THE WORLD | MAN FROM HEAVEN | BLESSING FOR ALL PEOPLE
GENEROUS PROVIDER | PERFECT SACRIFICE

WEEK 02

DAY 08

THE
SECOND
SUNDAY OF
ADVENT

FOR MY EYES HAVE SEEN YOUR SALVATION.
<u>YOU HAVE PREPARED IT
IN THE PRESENCE OF ALL PEOPLES.</u>

LUKE 2:30–31

We are using the first two Sundays of Advent to anticipate the hope of Jesus's arrival as we memorize our key passage together. This week we will add the second part of Luke 2:30–31, a reminder that Jesus was born to bring salvation to everyone.

BREAD OF LIFE,

WEEK 02

DAY 09

COME

EXODUS 16:1–12

MANNA AND QUAIL PROVIDED

¹ The entire Israelite community departed from Elim and came to the Wilderness of Sin, which is between Elim and Sinai, on the fifteenth day of the second month after they had left the land of Egypt. ² The entire Israelite community grumbled against Moses and Aaron in the wilderness. ³ The Israelites said to them, "If only we had died by the Lord's hand in the land of Egypt, when we sat by pots of meat and ate all the bread we wanted. Instead, you brought us into this wilderness to make this whole assembly die of hunger!"

⁴ Then the Lord said to Moses, "I am going to rain bread from heaven for you. The people are to go out each day and gather enough for that day. This way I will test them to see whether or not they will follow my instructions. ⁵ On the sixth day, when they prepare what they bring in, it will be twice as much as they gather on other days."

⁶ So Moses and Aaron said to all the Israelites, "This evening you will know that it was the Lord who brought you out of the land of Egypt, ⁷ and in the morning you will see the Lord's glory because he has heard your complaints about him. For who are we that you complain about us?" ⁸ Moses continued, "The Lord will give you meat to eat this evening and all the bread you want in the morning, for he has heard the complaints that you are raising against him. Who are we? Your complaints are not against us but against the Lord."

⁹ Then Moses told Aaron, "Say to the entire Israelite community, 'Come before the Lord, for he has heard your complaints.'" ¹⁰ As Aaron was speaking to the entire Israelite community, they turned toward the wilderness, and there in a cloud the Lord's glory appeared.

¹¹ The Lord spoke to Moses, ¹² "I have heard the complaints of the Israelites. Tell them: At twilight you will eat meat, and in the morning you will eat bread until you are full. Then you will know that I am the Lord your God."

JOHN 6:22–40, 56–58

THE BREAD OF LIFE

²² The next day, the crowd that had stayed on the other side of the sea saw there had been only one boat. They also saw that Jesus had not boarded the boat with his disciples, but that his disciples had gone off alone. ²³ Some boats from Tiberias came near the place where they had eaten the bread after the Lord had given thanks. ²⁴ When the crowd saw that neither Jesus nor his disciples were there, they got into the boats and went to Capernaum looking for Jesus. ²⁵ When they found him on the other side of the sea, they said to him, "Rabbi, when did you get here?"

²⁶ Jesus answered, "Truly I tell you, you are looking for me, not because you saw the signs, but because you ate the loaves and were filled. ²⁷ Don't work for the food that perishes but for the food that lasts for eternal life, which the Son of Man will give you, because God the Father has set his seal of approval on him."

²⁸ "What can we do to perform the works of God?" they asked.

²⁹ Jesus replied, "This is the work of God—that you believe in the one he has sent."

³⁰ "What sign, then, are you going to do so that we may see and believe you?" they asked. "What are you going to perform? ³¹ Our ancestors ate the manna in the wilderness, just as it is written: He gave them bread from heaven to eat."

³² Jesus said to them, "Truly I tell you, Moses didn't give you the bread from heaven, but my Father gives you the true bread from heaven. ³³ For the bread of God is the one who comes down from heaven and gives life to the world."

³⁴ Then they said, "Sir, give us this bread always."

³⁵ "I am the bread of life," Jesus told them. "No one who comes to me will ever be hungry, and no one who believes in me will ever be thirsty again. ³⁶ But as I told you, you've seen me, and yet you do not believe. ³⁷ Everyone the Father gives me will come to me, and the one who comes to me I will never cast out. ³⁸ For I have come down from heaven, not to do my own will, but the will of him who sent me. ³⁹ This is the will of him who sent me: that I should lose none of those he has given me but should raise them up on the last day.

⁴⁰ FOR THIS IS THE WILL OF MY FATHER: THAT EVERYONE WHO SEES THE SON AND BELIEVES IN HIM WILL HAVE ETERNAL LIFE, AND I WILL RAISE HIM UP ON THE LAST DAY."

...

⁵⁶ "The one who eats my flesh and drinks my blood remains in me, and I in him. ⁵⁷ Just as the living Father sent me and I live because of the Father, so the one who feeds on me will live because of me. ⁵⁸ This is the bread that came down from heaven; it is not like the manna your ancestors ate—and they died. The one who eats this bread will live forever."

PAUSE

DATE / /

In what ways have I seen or experienced Jesus as the Bread of Life in the past?

In what ways do I long to see Jesus as the Bread of Life in my life now?

& REFLECT

WEEK 02

LIVING WATER, COME

DAY 10

NOTES

EXODUS 17:1-7

WATER FROM THE ROCK

¹ The entire Israelite community left the Wilderness of Sin, moving from one place to the next according to the Lord's command. They camped at Rephidim, but there was no water for the people to drink. ² So the people complained to Moses, "Give us water to drink."

"Why are you complaining to me?" Moses replied to them. "Why are you testing the Lord?"

³ But the people thirsted there for water and grumbled against Moses. They said, "Why did you ever bring us up from Egypt to kill us and our children and our livestock with thirst?"

⁴ Then Moses cried out to the Lord, "What should I do with these people? In a little while they will stone me!"

⁵ The Lord answered Moses, "Go on ahead of the people and take some of the elders of Israel with you. Take the staff you struck the Nile with in your hand and go. ⁶ I am going to stand there in front of you on the rock at Horeb; when you hit the rock, water will come out of it and the people will drink." Moses did this in the sight of the elders of Israel. ⁷ He named the place Massah and Meribah because the Israelites complained, and because they tested the Lord, saying, "Is the Lord among us or not?"

JOHN 4:1-26

JESUS AND THE SAMARITAN WOMAN

¹ When Jesus learned that the Pharisees had heard he was making and baptizing more disciples than John ² (though Jesus himself was not baptizing, but his disciples were), ³ he left Judea and went again to Galilee. ⁴ He had to travel through Samaria; ⁵ so he came to a town of Samaria called Sychar near the property that Jacob had given his son Joseph. ⁶ Jacob's well was there, and Jesus, worn out from his journey, sat down at the well. It was about noon.

⁷ A woman of Samaria came to draw water.

"Give me a drink," Jesus said to her, ⁸ because his disciples had gone into town to buy food.

⁹ "How is it that you, a Jew, ask for a drink from me, a Samaritan woman?" she asked him. For Jews do not associate with Samaritans.

¹⁰ Jesus answered,

"IF YOU KNEW THE GIFT OF GOD, AND WHO IS SAYING TO YOU, 'GIVE ME A DRINK,' YOU WOULD ASK HIM, AND HE WOULD GIVE YOU LIVING WATER."

¹¹ "Sir," said the woman, "you don't even have a bucket, and the well is deep. So where do you get this 'living water'? ¹² You aren't greater than our father Jacob, are you? He gave us the well and drank from it himself, as did his sons and livestock."

¹³ Jesus said, "Everyone who drinks from this water will get thirsty again. ¹⁴ But whoever drinks from the water that I will give him will never get thirsty again. In fact, the water I will give him will become a well of water springing up in him for eternal life."

¹⁵ "Sir," the woman said to him, "give me this water so that I won't get thirsty and come here to draw water."

¹⁶ "Go call your husband," he told her, "and come back here."

¹⁷ "I don't have a husband," she answered.

"You have correctly said, 'I don't have a husband,'" Jesus said. ¹⁸ "For you've had five husbands, and the man you now have is not your husband. What you have said is true."

¹⁹ "Sir," the woman replied, "I see that you are a prophet. ²⁰ Our ancestors worshiped on this mountain, but you Jews say that the place to worship is in Jerusalem."

NOTES

[21] Jesus told her, "Believe me, woman, an hour is coming when you will worship the Father neither on this mountain nor in Jerusalem. [22] You Samaritans worship what you do not know. We worship what we do know, because salvation is from the Jews. [23] But an hour is coming, and is now here, when the true worshipers will worship the Father in Spirit and in truth. Yes, the Father wants such people to worship him. [24] God is spirit, and those who worship him must worship in Spirit and in truth."

[25] The woman said to him, "I know that the Messiah is coming" (who is called Christ). "When he comes, he will explain everything to us."

[26] Jesus told her, "I, the one speaking to you, am he."

JOHN 7:37–39

THE PROMISE OF THE SPIRIT

[37] On the last and most important day of the festival, Jesus stood up and cried out, "If anyone is thirsty, let him come to me and drink.

[38] THE ONE WHO BELIEVES IN ME, AS THE SCRIPTURE HAS SAID, WILL HAVE STREAMS OF LIVING WATER FLOW FROM DEEP WITHIN HIM."

[39] He said this about the Spirit. Those who believed in Jesus were going to receive the Spirit, for the Spirit had not yet been given because Jesus had not yet been glorified.

REVELATION 21:5–7

[5] Then the one seated on the throne said, "Look, I am making everything new." He also said, "Write, because these words are faithful and true." [6] Then he said to me, "It is done! I am the Alpha and the Omega, the beginning and the end. I will freely give to the thirsty from the spring of the water of life. [7] The one who conquers will inherit these things, and I will be his God, and he will be my son."

REVELATION 22:17

Both the Spirit and the bride say, "Come!" Let anyone who hears, say, "Come!" Let the one who is thirsty come. Let the one who desires take the water of life freely.

PAUSE

DATE / /

In what ways have I seen or experienced Jesus as the living water in the past?

In what ways do I long to see Jesus as the living water in my life now?

RESTORER

DAY ELEVEN

OF

LIFE,

COME

NUMBERS 21:4-9

THE BRONZE SNAKE

⁴ Then they set out from Mount Hor by way of the Red Sea to bypass the land of Edom, but the people became impatient because of the journey. ⁵ The people spoke against God and Moses: "Why have you led us up from Egypt to die in the wilderness? There is no bread or water, and we detest this wretched food!" ⁶ Then the Lord sent poisonous snakes among the people, and they bit them so that many Israelites died.

⁷ The people then came to Moses and said, "We have sinned by speaking against the Lord and against you. Intercede with the Lord so that he will take the snakes away from us." And Moses interceded for the people.

⁸ Then the Lord said to Moses, "Make a snake image and mount it on a pole. When anyone who is bitten looks at it, he will recover." ⁹ So Moses made a bronze snake and mounted it on a pole. Whenever someone was bitten, and he looked at the bronze snake, he recovered.

JOHN 3:1-15

JESUS AND NICODEMUS

¹ There was a man from the Pharisees named Nicodemus, a ruler of the Jews. ² This man came to him at night and said, "Rabbi, we know that you are a teacher who has come from God, for no one could perform these signs you do unless God were with him."

³ Jesus replied, "Truly I tell you, unless someone is born again, he cannot see the kingdom of God."

⁴ "How can anyone be born when he is old?" Nicodemus asked him. "Can he enter his mother's womb a second time and be born?"

⁵ Jesus answered, "Truly I tell you, unless someone is born of water and the Spirit, he cannot enter the kingdom of God.

NOTES

⁶ Whatever is born of the flesh is flesh, and whatever is born of the Spirit is spirit. ⁷ Do not be amazed that I told you that you must be born again. ⁸ The wind blows where it pleases, and you hear its sound, but you don't know where it comes from or where it is going. So it is with everyone born of the Spirit."

⁹ "How can these things be?" asked Nicodemus.

¹⁰ "Are you a teacher of Israel and don't know these things?" Jesus replied. ¹¹ "Truly I tell you, we speak what we know and we testify to what we have seen, but you do not accept our testimony. ¹² If I have told you about earthly things and you don't believe, how will you believe if I tell you about heavenly things? ¹³ No one has ascended into heaven except the one who descended from heaven —the Son of Man.

¹⁴ "Just as Moses lifted up the snake in the wilderness, so the Son of Man must be lifted up, ¹⁵ so that everyone who believes in him may have eternal life."

1 PETER 2:22-24

²² He did not commit sin, and no deceit was found in his mouth; ²³ when he was insulted, he did not insult in return; when he suffered, he did not threaten but entrusted himself to the one who judges justly. ²⁴ He himself bore our sins in his body on the tree; so that, having died to sins,

WE MIGHT LIVE FOR RIGHTEOUSNESS.

By his wounds you have been healed.

PAUSE

DATE / /

In what ways have I seen or experienced Jesus as the restorer of life in the past?

In what ways do I long to see Jesus as the restorer of life in my life now?

RIGHTEOUS MEDIATOR, COME

DAY 12

> "INSTEAD, THIS IS THE COVENANT I WILL MAKE WITH THE HOUSE OF ISRAEL AFTER THOSE DAYS"—THE LORD'S DECLARATION. "I WILL PUT MY TEACHING WITHIN THEM AND WRITE IT ON THEIR HEARTS. I WILL BE THEIR GOD, AND THEY WILL BE MY PEOPLE."
>
> JEREMIAH 31:33

DEUTERONOMY 6:1-25

THE GREATEST COMMAND

¹ This is the command—the statutes and ordinances—the LORD your God has commanded me to teach you, so that you may follow them in the land you are about to enter and possess. ² Do this so that you may fear the LORD your God all the days of your life by keeping all his statutes and commands I am giving you, your son, and your grandson, and so that you may have a long life. ³ Listen, Israel, and be careful to follow them, so that you may prosper and multiply greatly, because the LORD, the God of your ancestors, has promised you a land flowing with milk and honey.

⁴ Listen, Israel: The LORD our God, the LORD is one.

⁵ **LOVE THE LORD YOUR GOD WITH ALL YOUR HEART, WITH ALL YOUR SOUL, AND WITH ALL YOUR STRENGTH.**

⁶ These words that I am giving you today are to be in your heart. ⁷ Repeat them to your children. Talk about them when you sit in your house and when you walk along the road, when you lie down and when you get up. ⁸ Bind them as a sign on your hand and let them be a symbol on your forehead. ⁹ Write them on the doorposts of your house and on your city gates.

REMEMBERING GOD THROUGH OBEDIENCE

¹⁰ When the LORD your God brings you into the land he swore to your ancestors Abraham, Isaac, and Jacob that he would give you—a land with large and beautiful cities that you did not build, ¹¹ houses full of every good thing that you did not fill them with, cisterns that you did not dig, and vineyards and olive groves that you did not plant—and when you eat and are satisfied, ¹² be careful not to forget the LORD who brought you out of the land of Egypt, out of the place of slavery. ¹³ Fear the LORD your God, worship him, and take your oaths in his name. ¹⁴ Do not follow other gods, the gods of the peoples around you, ¹⁵ for the LORD your God, who is among you, is a jealous God. Otherwise, the LORD your God will become angry with you and obliterate you from the face of the earth. ¹⁶ Do not test the LORD your God as you tested him at Massah. ¹⁷ Carefully observe the commands of the LORD your God, the decrees and statutes he has commanded you. ¹⁸ Do what is right and good in the LORD's sight, so that you may prosper and so that you may enter and possess the good land the LORD your God swore to give your ancestors, ¹⁹ by driving out all your enemies before you, as the LORD has said.

²⁰ When your son asks you in the future, "What is the meaning of the decrees, statutes, and ordinances that the LORD our God has commanded you?" ²¹ tell him, "We were slaves of Pharaoh in Egypt, but the LORD brought us out of Egypt with a strong hand. ²² Before our eyes the LORD inflicted great and devastating signs and wonders on Egypt, on Pharaoh, and on all his household, ²³ but he brought us from there in order to lead us in and give us the land that he swore to our ancestors. ²⁴ The LORD commanded us to follow all these statutes and to fear the LORD our God for our prosperity always and for our preservation, as it is today. ²⁵ Righteousness will be ours if we are careful to follow every one of these commands before the LORD our God, as he has commanded us."

JEREMIAH 31:31-34

THE NEW COVENANT

[31] "Look, the days are coming"—this is the Lord's declaration—"when I will make a new covenant with the house of Israel and with the house of Judah. [32] This one will not be like the covenant I made with their ancestors on the day I took them by the hand to lead them out of the land of Egypt—my covenant that they broke even though I am their master"—the Lord's declaration. [33] "Instead, this is the covenant I will make with the house of Israel after those days"—the Lord's declaration. "I will put my teaching within them and write it on their hearts. I will be their God, and they will be my people. [34] No longer will one teach his neighbor or his brother, saying, 'Know the Lord,' for they will all know me, from the least to the greatest of them"—this is the Lord's declaration. "For I will forgive their iniquity and never again remember their sin."

MATTHEW 5:17

"Don't think that I came to abolish the Law or the Prophets. I did not come to abolish but to fulfill."

LUKE 22:14-20

THE FIRST LORD'S SUPPER

[14] When the hour came, he reclined at the table, and the apostles with him. [15] Then he said to them, "I have fervently desired to eat this Passover with you before I suffer. [16] For I tell you, I will not eat it again until it is fulfilled in the kingdom of God." [17] Then he took a cup, and after giving thanks, he said, "Take this and share it among yourselves. [18] For I tell you, from now on I will not drink of the fruit of the vine until the kingdom of God comes."

[19] And he took bread, gave thanks, broke it, gave it to them, and said, "This is my body, which is given for you. Do this in remembrance of me."

[20] In the same way he also took the cup after supper and said,

"THIS CUP IS THE NEW COVENANT IN MY BLOOD, WHICH IS POURED OUT FOR YOU."

PAUSE

DATE / /

In what ways have I seen or experienced Jesus as the righteous Mediator in the past?

In what ways do I long to see Jesus as the righteous Mediator in my life now?

RECIPE

ALL-DAY SPICED CIDER

MAKES: _10 servings_

INGREDIENTS

8 cups apple juice

4 cups cranberry juice

1 apple, sliced

1 orange, sliced

Cloves

Whole cinnamon sticks

INSTRUCTIONS

Pour all the juices into a large dutch oven over medium heat. Insert cloves into apple and orange slices. Place the apple slices, orange slices, and whole cinnamon sticks in the dutch oven (they should remain floating). Mull on medium to low heat for 2 to 3 hours. Just before guests arrive, increase the temperature so it steams. Ladle into mugs and garnish with a cinnamon stick.

DAY 13

GREAT HIGH PRIEST, COME

LEVITICUS 9:1-7

THE PRIESTLY MINISTRY INAUGURATED

¹ On the eighth day Moses summoned Aaron, his sons, and the elders of Israel. ² He said to Aaron, "Take a young bull for a sin offering and a ram for a burnt offering, both without blemish, and present them before the Lord. ³ And tell the Israelites: Take a male goat for a sin offering; a calf and a lamb, male yearlings without blemish, for a burnt offering; ⁴ an ox and a ram for a fellowship offering to sacrifice before the Lord; and a grain offering mixed with oil. For today the Lord is going to appear to you."

⁵ They brought what Moses had commanded to the front of the tent of meeting, and the whole community came forward and stood before the Lord. ⁶ Moses said, "This is what the Lord commanded you to do, that the glory of the Lord may appear to you." ⁷ Then Moses said to Aaron, "Approach the altar and sacrifice your sin offering and your burnt offering; make atonement for yourself and the people. Sacrifice the people's offering and make atonement for them, as the Lord commanded."

LEVITICUS 16:29-34

²⁹ "This is to be a permanent statute for you: In the seventh month, on the tenth day of the month you are to practice self-denial and do no work, both the native and the alien who resides among you. ³⁰ Atonement will be made for you on this day to cleanse you, and you will be clean from all your sins before the Lord. ³¹ It is a Sabbath of complete rest for you, and you must practice self-denial; it is a permanent statute. ³² The priest who is anointed and ordained to serve as high priest in place of his father will make atonement. He will put on the linen garments, the holy garments, ³³ and make atonement for the most holy place. He will make atonement for the tent of meeting and the altar and will make atonement for the priests and all the people of the assembly. ³⁴ This is to be a permanent statute for you, to make atonement for the Israelites once a year because of all their sins." And all this was done as the Lord commanded Moses.

HEBREWS 4:14-16

OUR GREAT HIGH PRIEST

¹⁴ Therefore, since we have a great high priest who has passed through the heavens—Jesus the Son of God—let us hold fast to our confession.

¹⁵ **FOR WE DO NOT HAVE A HIGH PRIEST WHO IS UNABLE TO SYMPATHIZE WITH OUR WEAKNESSES, BUT ONE WHO HAS BEEN TEMPTED IN EVERY WAY AS WE ARE, YET WITHOUT SIN.**

¹⁶ Therefore, let us approach the throne of grace with boldness, so that we may receive mercy and find grace to help us in time of need.

HEBREWS 5:1-10

CHRIST, A HIGH PRIEST

¹ For every high priest taken from among men is appointed in matters pertaining to God for the people, to offer both gifts and sacrifices for sins. ² He is able to deal gently with those who are ignorant and are going astray, since he is

also clothed with weakness. ³ Because of this, he must make an offering for his own sins as well as for the people. ⁴ No one takes this honor on himself; instead, a person is called by God, just as Aaron was. ⁵ In the same way, Christ did not exalt himself to become a high priest, but God who said to him,

> You are my Son;
> today I have become your Father,

⁶ also says in another place,

> You are a priest forever
> according to the order of Melchizedek.

⁷ During his earthly life, he offered prayers and appeals with loud cries and tears to the one who was able to save him from death, and he was heard because of his reverence. ⁸ Although he was the Son, he learned obedience from what he suffered. ⁹ After he was perfected, he became the source of eternal salvation for all who obey him, ¹⁰ and he was declared by God a high priest according to the order of Melchizedek.

HEBREWS 10:11–14

¹¹ Every priest stands day after day ministering and offering the same sacrifices time after time, which can never take away sins. ¹² But this man, after offering one sacrifice for sins forever, sat down at the right hand of God. ¹³ He is now waiting until his enemies are made his footstool. ¹⁴ For by one offering he has perfected forever those who are sanctified.

PAUSE

DATE / /

In what ways have I seen or experienced Jesus as the Great High Priest in the past?

In what ways do I long to see Jesus as the Great High Priest in my life now?

& REFLECT

DAY 14

GRACE DAY

Take this day to catch up on your reading, pray, and rest in the presence of the Lord. Use the pages that follow to express any stirred longings, letting this week's Scripture guide your reflection.

The woman said to him, "I know that the Messiah is coming" (who is called Christ). "When he comes, he will explain everything to us."

John 4:25

RESPONSE

Write a prayer of gratitude, thanking Jesus for who He is.

I praise you, Jesus, for being the _____

_____
_____
_____
_____
_____
_____
_____
_____
_____
_____
_____
_____
_____

WEEK 02

**BREAD OF LIFE | LIVING WATER | RESTORER OF LIFE
RIGHTEOUS MEDIATOR | GREAT HIGH PRIEST**

DATE / /

Write a prayer of longing, expressing your desire to see this aspect of Jesus in your life.

Come, _____

_____
_____
_____
_____
_____
_____
_____
_____
_____
_____
_____
_____
_____

BREAD OF LIFE | LIVING WATER | RESTORER OF LIFE
RIGHTEOUS MEDIATOR | GREAT HIGH PRIEST

WEEK 03

DAY 15

THE
THIRD
SUNDAY OF
ADVENT

**HOW COUNTLESS ARE YOUR WORKS, LORD!
IN WISDOM YOU HAVE MADE THEM ALL;
THE EARTH IS FULL OF YOUR CREATURES.**

PSALM 104:24

The first two weeks of our reading plan have explored the unique ways Jesus was the answer to generations of hope, expectation, and longing. On this third Sunday of Advent, we enter into the final days of anticipation for Christmas Day. This week, we'll read one O Antiphon prayer each day—along with our daily reading—to guide us to Christmas and the celebration of Jesus who has indeed come to us.

**O WISDOM, COMING FORTH FROM THE MOUTH
OF THE MOST HIGH,
REACHING FROM ONE END TO THE OTHER,
MIGHTILY AND SWEETLY ORDERING ALL THINGS:
COME AND TEACH US THE WAY OF PRUDENCE.**

LORD,
COME

DAY 16

O LORD, AND LEADER OF THE HOUSE OF ISRAEL,
WHO APPEARED TO MOSES IN THE FIRE
OF THE BURNING BUSH
AND GAVE HIM THE LAW ON SINAI:
COME AND REDEEM US WITH AN OUTSTRETCHED ARM.

JOHN 5:37-47

37 "The Father who sent me has himself testified about me. You have not heard his voice at any time, and you haven't seen his form. 38 You don't have his word residing in you, because you don't believe the one he sent. 39 You pore over the Scriptures because you think you have eternal life in them, and yet they testify about me. 40 But you are not willing to come to me so that you may have life.

41 "I do not accept glory from people, 42 but I know you—that you have no love for God within you. 43 I have come in my Father's name, and yet you don't accept me. If someone else comes in his own name, you will accept him. 44 How can you believe, since you accept glory from one another but don't seek the glory that comes from the only God? 45 Do not think that I will accuse you to the Father. Your accuser is Moses, on whom you have set your hope. 46 For if you believed Moses, you would believe me, because he wrote about me. 47 But if you don't believe what he wrote, how will you believe my words?"

EXODUS 3:1-16

MOSES AND THE BURNING BUSH

1 Meanwhile, Moses was shepherding the flock of his father-in-law Jethro, the priest of Midian. He led the flock to the far side of the wilderness and came to Horeb, the mountain of God. 2 Then the angel of the LORD appeared to him in a flame of fire within a bush. As Moses looked, he saw that the bush was on fire but was not consumed. 3 So Moses thought, "I must go over and look at this remarkable sight. Why isn't the bush burning up?"

⁴ When the LORD saw that he had gone over to look, God called out to him from the bush, "Moses, Moses!"

"Here I am," he answered.

⁵ "Do not come closer," he said. "Remove the sandals from your feet, for the place where you are standing is holy ground." ⁶ Then he continued, "I am the God of your father, the God of Abraham, the God of Isaac, and the God of Jacob." Moses hid his face because he was afraid to look at God.

⁷ Then the LORD said, "I have observed the misery of my people in Egypt, and have heard them crying out because of their oppressors. I know about their sufferings, ⁸ and I have come down to rescue them from the power of the Egyptians and to bring them from that land to a good and spacious land, a land flowing with milk and honey—the territory of the Canaanites, Hethites, Amorites, Perizzites, Hivites, and Jebusites. ⁹ So because the Israelites' cry for help has come to me, and I have also seen the way the Egyptians are oppressing them, ¹⁰ therefore, go. I am sending you to Pharaoh so that you may lead my people, the Israelites, out of Egypt."

¹¹ But Moses asked God, "Who am I that I should go to Pharaoh and that I should bring the Israelites out of Egypt?"

¹² He answered, "I will certainly be with you, and this will be the sign to you that I am the one who sent you: when you bring the people out of Egypt, you will all worship God at this mountain."

¹³ Then Moses asked God, "If I go to the Israelites and say to them, 'The God of your ancestors has sent me to you,' and they ask me, 'What is his name?' what should I tell them?"

¹⁴ God replied to Moses, "I AM WHO I AM. This is what you are to say to the Israelites: I AM has sent me to you." ¹⁵ God also said to Moses, "Say this to the Israelites: The LORD, the God of your ancestors, the God of Abraham, the God of Isaac, and the God of Jacob, has sent me to you. This

is my name forever; this is how I am to be remembered in every generation.

¹⁶ "Go and assemble the elders of Israel and say to them: The Lord, the God of your ancestors, the God of Abraham, Isaac, and Jacob, has appeared to me and said: I have paid close attention to you and to what has been done to you in Egypt."

ISAIAH 33:22

For the Lord is our Judge,
the Lord is our Lawgiver,
the Lord is our King.
He will save us.

PHILIPPIANS 2:5-11

CHRIST'S HUMILITY AND EXALTATION

⁵ Adopt the same attitude as that of Christ Jesus,

> ⁶ who, existing in the form of God,
> did not consider equality with God
> as something to be exploited.
> ⁷ Instead he emptied himself
> by assuming the form of a servant,
> taking on the likeness of humanity.
> And when he had come as a man,
> ⁸ he humbled himself by becoming obedient
> to the point of death—
> even to death on a cross.
> ⁹ For this reason God highly exalted him
> and gave him the name
> that is above every name,
> ¹⁰ so that at the name of Jesus
> every knee will bow—
> in heaven and on earth
> and under the earth—
> ¹¹ and every tongue will confess
> that Jesus Christ is Lord,
> to the glory of God the Father.

PAUSE

DATE / /

> Use this space to pause and reflect on your Scripture reading.
> Let today's O Antiphon prayer deepen your celebration of Jesus's birth.

& REFLECT

ROOT OF JESSE,

WEEK 03

DAY 17

COME

> O ROOT OF JESSE, STANDING AS A SIGN AMONG
> THE PEOPLES;
> BEFORE YOU KINGS WILL SHUT THEIR MOUTHS,
> TO YOU THE NATIONS WILL MAKE THEIR PRAYER:
> COME AND DELIVER US, AND DELAY NO LONGER.

JEREMIAH 23:5-6

THE RIGHTEOUS BRANCH OF DAVID

⁵ "Look, the days are coming"—this is the Lord's declaration—
"when I will raise up a Righteous Branch for David.
He will reign wisely as king
and administer justice and righteousness in the land.

⁶ In his days Judah will be saved,
and Israel will dwell securely.
This is the name he will be called:
The Lord Is Our Righteousness."

ISAIAH 11:1-10

REIGN OF THE DAVIDIC KING

¹ Then a shoot will grow from the stump of Jesse,
and a branch from his roots will bear fruit.
² The Spirit of the Lord will rest on him—
a Spirit of wisdom and understanding,
a Spirit of counsel and strength,
a Spirit of knowledge and of the fear of the Lord.
³ His delight will be in the fear of the Lord.
He will not judge
by what he sees with his eyes,
he will not execute justice
by what he hears with his ears,
⁴ but he will judge the poor righteously
and execute justice for the oppressed of the land.
He will strike the land
with a scepter from his mouth,
and he will kill the wicked
with a command from his lips.
⁵ Righteousness will be a belt around his hips;
faithfulness will be a belt around his waist.

⁶ The wolf will dwell with the lamb,
and the leopard will lie down with the goat.
The calf, the young lion, and the fattened
    calf will be together,
and a child will lead them.
⁷ The cow and the bear will graze,
their young ones will lie down together,
and the lion will eat straw like cattle.
⁸ An infant will play beside the cobra's pit,
and a toddler will put his hand into a
    snake's den.
⁹ They will not harm or destroy each other
on my entire holy mountain,
for the land will be as full
of the knowledge of the Lord
as the sea is filled with water.

ISRAEL REGATHERED

¹⁰ On that day the root of Jesse
will stand as a banner for the peoples.
The nations will look to him for guidance,
and his resting place will be glorious.

PSALM 57:2-3

² I call to God Most High,
to God who fulfills his purpose for me.
³ He reaches down from heaven and saves me,
challenging the one who tramples me.   *Selah*
God sends his faithful love and truth.

ROMANS 15:4-13

⁴ For whatever was written in the past was written for our instruction, so that we may have hope through endurance and through the encouragement from the Scriptures. ⁵ Now may the God who gives endurance and encouragement grant you to live in harmony with one another, according to Christ Jesus, ⁶ so that you may glorify the God and Father of our Lord Jesus Christ with one mind and one voice.

GLORIFYING GOD TOGETHER

⁷ Therefore welcome one another, just as Christ also welcomed you, to the glory of God. ⁸ For I say that Christ became a servant of the circumcised on behalf of God's truth, to confirm the promises to the fathers, ⁹ and so that Gentiles may glorify God for his mercy. As it is written,

> Therefore I will praise you among
>   the Gentiles,
> and I will sing praise to your name.

¹⁰ Again it says, Rejoice, you Gentiles, with his people! ¹¹ And again,

> Praise the Lord, all you Gentiles;
> let all the peoples praise him!

¹² And again, Isaiah says,

> The root of Jesse will appear,
> the one who rises to rule the Gentiles;
> the Gentiles will hope in him.

¹³ Now may the God of hope fill you with all joy and peace as you believe so that you may overflow with hope by the power of the Holy Spirit.

REVELATION 5:5

Then one of the elders said to me, "Do not weep. Look, the Lion from the tribe of Judah, the Root of David, has conquered so that he is able to open the scroll and its seven seals."

PAUSE

DATE / /

> Use this space to pause and reflect on your Scripture reading.
> Let today's O Antiphon prayer deepen your celebration of Jesus's birth.

& REFLECT

KEY OF DAVID, COME

**O KEY OF DAVID AND SCEPTRE
OF THE HOUSE OF ISRAEL;
YOU OPEN AND NO ONE CAN SHUT;
YOU SHUT AND NO ONE CAN OPEN:
COME AND LEAD THE PRISONERS
FROM THE PRISON HOUSE,
THOSE WHO DWELL IN DARKNESS
AND THE SHADOW OF DEATH.**

NOTES

2 SAMUEL 7:8-16

⁸ "So now this is what you are to say to my servant David: 'This is what the Lord of Armies says: I took you from the pasture, from tending the flock, to be ruler over my people Israel. ⁹ I have been with you wherever you have gone, and I have destroyed all your enemies before you. I will make a great name for you like that of the greatest on the earth. ¹⁰ I will designate a place for my people Israel and plant them, so that they may live there and not be disturbed again. Evildoers will not continue to oppress them as they have done ¹¹ ever since the day I ordered judges to be over my people Israel. I will give you rest from all your enemies.

"'The Lord declares to you: The Lord himself will make a house for you. ¹² When your time comes and you rest with your ancestors, I will raise up after you your descendant, who will come from your body, and I will establish his kingdom. ¹³ He is the one who will build a house for my name, and I will establish the throne of his kingdom forever. ¹⁴ I will be his father, and he will be my son. When he does wrong, I will discipline him with a rod of men and blows from mortals. ¹⁵ But my faithful love will never leave him as it did when I removed it from Saul, whom I removed from before you. ¹⁶ Your house and kingdom will endure before me forever, and your throne will be established forever.'"

ISAIAH 52:7-10

⁷ How beautiful on the mountains
are the feet of the herald,
who proclaims peace,
who brings news of good things,
who proclaims salvation,
who says to Zion, "Your God reigns!"
⁸ The voices of your watchmen—
they lift up their voices,

shouting for joy together;
for every eye will see
when the LORD returns to Zion.
⁹ Be joyful, rejoice together,
you ruins of Jerusalem!
For the LORD has comforted his people;
he has redeemed Jerusalem.
¹⁰ The LORD has displayed his holy arm
in the sight of all the nations;
all the ends of the earth will see
the salvation of our God.

JOHN 12:12-13

THE TRIUMPHAL ENTRY

¹² The next day, when the large crowd that had come to the festival heard that Jesus was coming to Jerusalem, ¹³ they took palm branches and went out to meet him. They kept shouting:

> "*Hosanna!*
> Blessed is he who comes in the name of the Lord—the King of Israel!"

REVELATION 3:7-8

⁷ "Write to the angel of the church in Philadelphia: Thus says the Holy One, the true one, the one who has the key of David, who opens and no one will close, and who closes and no one opens: ⁸ I know your works. Look, I have placed before you an open door that no one can close because you have but little power; yet you have kept my word and have not denied my name."

REVELATION 1:12-18

¹² Then I turned to see whose voice it was that spoke to me. When I turned I saw seven golden lampstands, ¹³ and among the lampstands was one like the Son of Man, dressed in a robe and with a golden sash wrapped around his chest. ¹⁴ The hair of his head was white as wool—white as snow—and his eyes like a fiery flame. ¹⁵ His feet were like fine bronze as it is fired in a furnace, and his voice like the sound of cascading waters. ¹⁶ He had seven stars in his right hand; a sharp double-edged sword came from his mouth, and his face was shining like the sun at full strength.

¹⁷ When I saw him, I fell at his feet like a dead man. He laid his right hand on me and said, "Don't be afraid. I am the First and the Last, ¹⁸ and the Living One. I was dead, but look—I am alive forever and ever, and I hold the keys of death and Hades."

PAUSE

DATE / /

> Use this space to pause and reflect on your Scripture reading.
> Let today's O Antiphon prayer deepen your celebration of Jesus's birth.

& REFLECT

CHRISTMAS

AND THE SEASONS OF THE CHURCH

The Advent season marks the beginning of the Church calendar year, a centuries-old way many Christian denominations order the year to intentionally remember and celebrate the redeeming work of Christ. Structured around the moving date of Easter Sunday and the fixed date of Christmas, the liturgical Church calendar consists of six seasons as well as ordinary time. Here is a brief explanation of the three seasons that are specifically connected to the birth of Jesus: Advent, Christmastide, and Epiphany.

ADVENT

WHAT IS IT?

A season of anticipating the celebration of Jesus's birth, while also anticipating His promised return. The term *advent* comes from a Latin word meaning "coming" or "arrival."

WHEN IS IT?

Four Sundays before Christmas Day through December 24.

HOW IS IT OBSERVED?

Many Christians mark the four Sundays during Advent by lighting one candle each Sunday, and a fifth candle on Christmas Eve. The colors of these candles vary between denominations, but many Protestant traditions use three purple or blue candles (the traditional Church color for Advent), one pink candle, and one white candle. The candles represent the themes of hope, peace, joy, love, and the light of Christ.

CHRISTMASTIDE

WHAT IS IT?

A season celebrating the birth of Jesus.

WHEN IS IT?

December 25 through January 5, also known as the Twelve Days of Christmas and Yuletide.

HOW IS IT OBSERVED?

Celebrations in this season revolve around rejoicing and remembering Jesus's birth; themes of joy, merriment, and goodwill mark Christmastide. Many Christians give gifts, go caroling, attend church services and Christmas nativity plays, and enjoy special meals with each other throughout the twelve-day celebration.

> **KEY SCRIPTURES**
>
> Is 9:2–7; Mt 1:18–25; Lk 1:26–38; 2:1–20

EPIPHANY

WHAT IS IT?

Epiphany comes from a Greek word that means "to manifest" or "to show." It is also known as the Feast of the Three Kings, Three Kings' Day, and Twelfth Night. Epiphany commemorates the arrival of the wise men to Bethlehem and is a reminder that Christ's birth is good news for all creation.

WHEN IS IT?

January 6, twelve days after Christmas. Some traditions celebrate Epiphany as a season through the Sunday before Ash Wednesday, rather than just one day.

HOW IS IT OBSERVED?

While the season is celebrated in different ways across various cultures and religious traditions, it commonly includes singing, attending church services, reciting blessings over homes, gift giving, and eating special food tied to the feast, such as the Three Kings' Cake.

> **KEY SCRIPTURE**
>
> Mt 2:1–12

WEEK 03

MORNING STAR, COME

DAY 19

NOTES

> O MORNING STAR,
> SPLENDOUR OF LIGHT ETERNAL
> AND SUN OF RIGHTEOUSNESS:
> COME AND ENLIGHTEN THOSE
> WHO DWELL IN DARKNESS AND
> THE SHADOW OF DEATH.

PSALM 78:1–8

LESSONS FROM ISRAEL'S PAST

A Maskil of Asaph.

¹ My people, hear my instruction;
listen to the words from my mouth.
² I will declare wise sayings;
I will speak mysteries from the past—
³ things we have heard and known
and that our ancestors have passed down to us.
⁴ We will not hide them from their children,
but will tell a future generation
the praiseworthy acts of the Lord,
his might, and the wondrous works
he has performed.
⁵ He established a testimony in Jacob
and set up a law in Israel,
which he commanded our ancestors
to teach to their children
⁶ so that a future generation—
children yet to be born—might know.
They were to rise and tell their children
⁷ so that they might put their confidence in God
and not forget God's works,
but keep his commands.
⁸ Then they would not be like their ancestors,
a stubborn and rebellious generation,
a generation whose heart was not loyal
and whose spirit was not faithful to God.

MALACHI 4:2

"But for you who fear my name, the sun of righteousness will rise with healing in its wings, and you will go out and playfully jump like calves from the stall."

MATTHEW 13:10-17, 34-35

WHY JESUS USED PARABLES

¹⁰ Then the disciples came up and asked him, "Why are you speaking to them in parables?"

¹¹ He answered, "Because the secrets of the kingdom of heaven have been given for you to know, but it has not been given to them. ¹² For whoever has, more will be given to him, and he will have more than enough; but whoever does not have, even what he has will be taken away from him. ¹³ That is why I speak to them in parables, because looking they do not see, and hearing they do not listen or understand. ¹⁴ Isaiah's prophecy is fulfilled in them, which says:

> You will listen and listen,
> but never understand;
> you will look and look,
> but never perceive.
> ¹⁵ For this people's heart has grown callous;
> their ears are hard of hearing,
> and they have shut their eyes;
> otherwise they might see with their eyes,
> and hear with their ears, and
> understand with their hearts,
> and turn back—
> and I would heal them.

¹⁶ "Blessed are your eyes because they do see, and your ears because they do hear. ¹⁷ For truly I tell you, many prophets and righteous people longed to see the things you see but didn't see them, to hear the things you hear but didn't hear them."

…

USING PARABLES FULFILLS PROPHECY

[34] Jesus told the crowds all these things in parables, and he did not tell them anything without a parable, [35] so that what was spoken through the prophet might be fulfilled:

> I will open my mouth in parables;
> I will declare things kept secret
> from the foundation of the world.

1 CORINTHIANS 1:20-25

[20] Where is the one who is wise? Where is the teacher of the law? Where is the debater of this age? Hasn't God made the world's wisdom foolish? [21] For since, in God's wisdom, the world did not know God through wisdom, God was pleased to save those who believe through the foolishness of what is preached. [22] For the Jews ask for signs and the Greeks seek wisdom, [23] but we preach Christ crucified, a stumbling block to the Jews and foolishness to the Gentiles. [24] Yet to those who are called, both Jews and Greeks, Christ is the power of God and the wisdom of God, [25] because God's foolishness is wiser than human wisdom, and God's weakness is stronger than human strength.

2 PETER 1:16-21

THE TRUSTWORTHY PROPHETIC WORD

[16] For we did not follow cleverly contrived myths when we made known to you the power and coming of our Lord Jesus Christ; instead, we were eyewitnesses of his majesty. [17] For he received honor and glory from God the Father when the voice came to him from the Majestic Glory, saying "This is my beloved Son, with whom I am well-pleased!" [18] We ourselves heard this voice when it came from heaven while we were with him on the holy mountain. [19] We also have the prophetic word strongly confirmed, and you will do well to pay attention to it, as to a lamp shining in a dark place, until the day dawns and the morning star rises in your hearts. [20] Above all, you know this: No prophecy of Scripture comes from the prophet's own interpretation, [21] because no prophecy ever came by the will of man; instead, men spoke from God as they were carried along by the Holy Spirit.

REVELATION 22:16

"I, Jesus, have sent my angel to attest these things to you for the churches. I am the Root and descendant of David, the bright morning star."

PAUSE

DATE / /

> Use this space to pause and reflect on your Scripture reading. Let today's O Antiphon prayer deepen your celebration of Jesus's birth.

KING OF

DAY TWENTY

THE

NATIONS,

COME

> **O KING OF THE NATIONS,**
> **AND THEIR DESIRE,**
> **THE CORNERSTONE MAKING BOTH ONE:**
> **COME AND SAVE THE HUMAN RACE,**
> **WHICH YOU FASHIONED FROM CLAY.**

EZEKIEL 36:16–38

RESTORATION OF ISRAEL'S PEOPLE

¹⁶ The word of the Lord came to me: ¹⁷ "Son of man, while the house of Israel lived in their land, they defiled it with their conduct and actions. Their behavior before me was like menstrual impurity. ¹⁸ So I poured out my wrath on them because of the blood they had shed on the land, and because they had defiled it with their idols. ¹⁹ I dispersed them among the nations, and they were scattered among the countries. I judged them according to their conduct and actions. ²⁰ When they came to the nations where they went, they profaned my holy name, because it was said about them, 'These are the people of the Lord, yet they had to leave his land in exile.' ²¹ Then I had concern for my holy name, which the house of Israel profaned among the nations where they went.

²² "Therefore, say to the house of Israel, 'This is what the Lord God says: It is not for your sake that I will act, house of Israel, but for my holy name, which you profaned among the nations where you went. ²³ I will honor the holiness of my great name, which has been profaned among the nations—the name you have profaned among them. The nations will know that I am the Lord—this is the declaration of the Lord God—when I demonstrate my holiness through you in their sight.

²⁴ "'For I will take you from the nations and gather you from all the countries, and will bring you into your own land. ²⁵ I will also sprinkle clean water on you, and you will be clean. I will cleanse you from all your impurities and all your idols.

²⁶ I WILL GIVE YOU A NEW HEART AND PUT A NEW SPIRIT WITHIN YOU; I WILL REMOVE YOUR HEART OF STONE AND GIVE YOU A HEART OF FLESH.

²⁷ I will place my Spirit within you and cause you to follow my statutes and carefully observe my ordinances. ²⁸ You will live in the land that I gave your ancestors; you will be my people, and I will be your God.

NOTES

²⁹ I will save you from all your uncleanness. I will summon the grain and make it plentiful, and I will not bring famine on you. ³⁰ I will also make the fruit of the trees and the produce of the field plentiful, so that you will no longer experience reproach among the nations on account of famine.

³¹ "'You will remember your evil ways and your deeds that were not good, and you will loathe yourselves for your iniquities and detestable practices. ³² It is not for your sake that I will act—this is the declaration of the Lord God—let this be known to you. Be ashamed and humiliated because of your ways, house of Israel!

³³ "'This is what the Lord God says: On the day I cleanse you from all your iniquities, I will cause the cities to be inhabited, and the ruins will be rebuilt. ³⁴ The desolate land will be cultivated instead of lying desolate in the sight of everyone who passes by. ³⁵ They will say, "This land that was desolate has become like the garden of Eden. The cities that were once ruined, desolate, and demolished are now fortified and inhabited." ³⁶ Then the nations that remain around you will know that I, the Lord, have rebuilt what was demolished and have replanted what was desolate. I, the Lord, have spoken and I will do it.

³⁷ "'This is what the Lord God says: I will respond to the house of Israel and do this for them: I will multiply them in number like a flock. ³⁸ So the ruined cities will be filled with a flock of people, just as Jerusalem is filled with a flock of sheep for sacrifice during its appointed festivals. Then they will know that I am the Lord.'"

ISAIAH 9:6–7

⁶ For a child will be born for us,
a son will be given to us,
and the government will be on his shoulders.
He will be named
Wonderful Counselor, Mighty God,
Eternal Father, Prince of Peace.
⁷ The dominion will be vast,
and its prosperity will never end.

He will reign on the throne of David
and over his kingdom,
to establish and sustain it
with justice and righteousness from now on and forever.
The zeal of the Lord of Armies will accomplish this.

JEREMIAH 10:7

Who should not fear you,
King of the nations?
It is what you deserve.
For among all the wise people of the nations
and among all their kingdoms,
there is no one like you.

LUKE 4:16–21

REJECTION AT NAZARETH

¹⁶ He came to Nazareth, where he had been brought up. As usual, he entered the synagogue on the Sabbath day and stood up to read. ¹⁷ The scroll of the prophet Isaiah was given to him, and unrolling the scroll, he found the place where it was written:

> ¹⁸ The Spirit of the Lord is on me,
> because he has anointed me
> to preach good news to the poor.
> He has sent me
> to proclaim release to the captives
> and recovery of sight to the blind,
> to set free the oppressed,
> ¹⁹ to proclaim the year of the Lord's favor.

²⁰ He then rolled up the scroll, gave it back to the attendant, and sat down. And the eyes of everyone in the synagogue were fixed on him. ²¹ He began by saying to them,

"TODAY AS YOU LISTEN, THIS SCRIPTURE HAS BEEN FULFILLED."

EPHESIANS 1:3–10

GOD'S RICH BLESSINGS

³ Blessed is the God and Father of our Lord Jesus Christ, who has blessed us with every spiritual blessing in the heavens in Christ. ⁴ For he chose us in him, before the foundation of the world, to be holy and blameless in love before him. ⁵ He predestined us to be adopted as sons through Jesus Christ for himself, according to the good pleasure of his will, ⁶ to the praise of his glorious grace that he lavished on us in the Beloved One.

⁷ In him we have redemption through his blood, the forgiveness of our trespasses, according to the riches of his grace ⁸ that he richly poured out on us with all wisdom and understanding. ⁹ He made known to us the mystery of his will, according to his good pleasure that he purposed in Christ ¹⁰ as a plan for the right time—to bring everything together in Christ, both things in heaven and things on earth in him.

PAUSE

DATE / /

> Use this space to pause and reflect on your Scripture reading.
> Let today's O Antiphon prayer deepen your celebration of Jesus's birth.

& REFLECT

DAY 20

GRACE DAY

DAY 21

Take this day to catch up on your reading, pray, and rest in the presence of the Lord.

> **O EMMANUEL, OUR KING AND OUR LAWGIVER,
> THE HOPE OF THE NATIONS AND THEIR SAVIOUR:
> COME AND SAVE US, O LORD OUR GOD.**

For the Lord is our Judge, the Lord is our Lawgiver, the Lord is our King. He will save us.

Isaiah 33:22

CHRISTMAS EVE

DAY — 22

IMMANUEL HAS COME

DAY 22

YOU WILL CONCEIVE AND GIVE
BIRTH TO A SON, AND YOU WILL
NAME HIM JESUS.

LUKE 1:31

LUKE 1:26-56

GABRIEL PREDICTS JESUS'S BIRTH

26 In the sixth month, the angel Gabriel was sent by God to a town in Galilee called Nazareth, 27 to a virgin engaged to a man named Joseph, of the house of David. The virgin's name was Mary. 28 And the angel came to her and said, "Greetings, favored woman! The Lord is with you." 29 But she was deeply troubled by this statement, wondering what kind of greeting this could be. 30 Then the angel told her, "Do not be afraid, Mary, for you have found favor with God. 31 Now listen: You will conceive and give birth to a son, and you will name him Jesus. 32 He will be great and will be called the Son of the Most High, and the Lord God will give him the throne of his father David. 33 He will reign over the house of Jacob forever, and his kingdom will have no end."

34 Mary asked the angel, "How can this be, since I have not had sexual relations with a man?"

35 The angel replied to her, "The Holy Spirit will come upon you, and the power of the Most High will overshadow you. Therefore, the holy one to be born will be called the Son of God. 36 And consider your relative Elizabeth—even she has conceived a son in her old age, and this is the sixth month for her who was called childless. 37 For nothing will be impossible with God."

38 "See, I am the Lord's servant," said Mary. "May it happen to me as you have said." Then the angel left her.

MARY'S VISIT TO ELIZABETH

39 In those days Mary set out and hurried to a town in the hill country of Judah 40 where she entered Zechariah's house and greeted Elizabeth. 41 When Elizabeth heard Mary's greeting, the baby leaped inside her, and Elizabeth was filled with the Holy Spirit. 42 Then she exclaimed with a loud cry, "Blessed are you among women, and your child will be blessed! 43 How could this happen to me, that the mother of my Lord should come to me? 44 For you see, when the sound of your greeting reached my ears, the baby leaped for joy inside me. 45 Blessed is she who has believed that the Lord would fulfill what he has spoken to her!"

MARY'S PRAISE

46 And Mary said:

> My soul magnifies the Lord,
> 47 and my spirit rejoices in God my Savior,
> 48 because he has looked with favor
> on the humble condition of his servant.
> Surely, from now on all generations
> will call me blessed,
> 49 because the Mighty One
> has done great things for me,
> and his name is holy.
> 50 His mercy is from generation
>   to generation
> on those who fear him.
> 51 He has done a mighty deed with his arm;
> he has scattered the proud
> because of the thoughts of their hearts;
> 52 he has toppled the mighty from
>   their thrones
> and exalted the lowly.
> 53 He has satisfied the hungry with
>   good things
> and sent the rich away empty.
> 54 He has helped his servant Israel,
> remembering his mercy

⁵⁵ to Abraham and his descendants forever,
just as he spoke to our ancestors.

⁵⁶ And Mary stayed with her about three months; then she returned to her home.

MATTHEW 1:18-25

THE NATIVITY OF THE MESSIAH

¹⁸ The birth of Jesus Christ came about this way: After his mother Mary had been engaged to Joseph, it was discovered before they came together that she was pregnant from the Holy Spirit. ¹⁹ So her husband, Joseph, being a righteous man, and not wanting to disgrace her publicly, decided to divorce her secretly.

²⁰ But after he had considered these things, an angel of the Lord appeared to him in a dream, saying, "Joseph, son of David, don't be afraid to take Mary as your wife, because what has been conceived in her is from the Holy Spirit. ²¹ She will give birth to a son, and you are to name him Jesus, because he will save his people from their sins."

²² Now all this took place to fulfill what was spoken by the Lord through the prophet:

²³ See, the virgin will become pregnant
and give birth to a son,
and they will name him Immanuel,

which is translated "God is with us."

²⁴ When Joseph woke up, he did as the Lord's angel had commanded him. He married her ²⁵ but did not have sexual relations with her until she gave birth to a son. And he named him Jesus.

ISAIAH 7:14

Therefore, the Lord himself will give you a sign: See, the virgin will conceive, have a son, and name him Immanuel.

PAUSE

DATE / /

> Use this space to pause and reflect on your Scripture reading.
> Let today's O Antiphon prayer deepen your celebration of Jesus's birth.

ANGELS, FROM THE REALMS OF GLORY

1. An-gels, from the realms of glo-ry, Wing your flight o'er all the earth;
2. Shep-herds, in the fields a-bid-ing, Watch-ing o'er your flocks by night,
3. Sag-es, leave your con-tem-pla-tions, Bright-er vi-sions beam a-far;
4. Saints be-fore the al-tar bend-ing, Watch-ing long in hope and fear,

Ye who sang cre-a-tion's sto-ry now pro-claim Mes-si-ah's birth:
God with man is now re-sid-ing, Yon-der shines the in-fant Light:
Seek the great de-sire of na-tions, Ye have seen the In-fant's star:
Sud-den-ly the Lord, de-scend-ing, In His tem-ple shall ap-pear:

Come and wor-ship, come and wor-ship, Wor-ship Christ, the new-born King!

WORDS: James Montgomery
MUSIC: Henry T. Smart
LAST STANZA: Bill Wolaver

CHRISTMAS DAY

DAY ———————————————— 23

THE SAVIOR OF THE WORLD

WEEK 04

DAY 23

HAS COME

LUKE 2:1-20

THE BIRTH OF JESUS

¹ In those days a decree went out from Caesar Augustus that the whole empire should be registered. ² This first registration took place while Quirinius was governing Syria. ³ So everyone went to be registered, each to his own town.

⁴ Joseph also went up from the town of Nazareth in Galilee, to Judea, to the city of David, which is called Bethlehem, because he was of the house and family line of David, ⁵ to be registered along with Mary, who was engaged to him and was pregnant. ⁶ While they were there, the time came for her to give birth. ⁷ Then she gave birth to her firstborn son, and she wrapped him tightly in cloth and laid him in a manger, because there was no guest room available for them.

THE SHEPHERDS AND THE ANGELS

⁸ In the same region, shepherds were staying out in the fields and keeping watch at night over their flock. ⁹ Then an angel of the Lord stood before them, and the glory of the Lord shone around them, and they were terrified. ¹⁰ But the angel said to them, "Don't be afraid, for look, I proclaim to you good news of great joy that will be for all the people: ¹¹ Today in the city of David a Savior was born for you, who is the Messiah, the Lord. ¹² This will be the sign for you: You will find a baby wrapped tightly in cloth and lying in a manger."

¹³ Suddenly there was a multitude of the heavenly host with the angel, praising God and saying:

> ¹⁴ Glory to God in the highest heaven,
> and peace on earth to people he favors!

¹⁵ When the angels had left them and returned to heaven, the shepherds said to one another, "Let's go straight to Bethlehem and see what has happened, which the Lord has made known to us."

[16] They hurried off and found both Mary and Joseph, and the baby who was lying in the manger. [17] After seeing them, they reported the message they were told about this child, [18] and all who heard it were amazed at what the shepherds said to them. [19] But Mary was treasuring up all these things in her heart and meditating on them. [20] The shepherds returned, glorifying and praising God for all the things they had seen and heard, which were just as they had been told.

GALATIANS 4:4-5

[4] When the time came to completion,

GOD SENT HIS SON, BORN OF A WOMAN, BORN UNDER THE LAW, [5] **TO REDEEM THOSE UNDER THE LAW, SO THAT WE MIGHT RECEIVE ADOPTION AS SONS.**

CHRISTMAS DAY REFLECTION

DATE ___/___/___

WHERE DID I SPEND CHRISTMAS DAY?

WHAT TIME DID I WAKE UP?

AM | PM

WHAT WAS THE WEATHER LIKE?
(circle one)

☀️ ☁️ 💧 ❄️

___° HIGH

___° LOW

WHO DID I CELEBRATE WITH?

WHAT SENSE OF LOSS, GRIEF, OR UNMET EXPECTATIONS DID I EXPERIENCE TODAY?

WHAT MADE ME LAUGH?

HOW DID I EXPERIENCE THE NEARNESS OF GOD TODAY?

What tradition meant the most to me this year?

HOW WAS CHRISTMAS DAY DIFFERENT THIS YEAR BECAUSE OF THE TIME I SPENT READING GOD'S WORD DURING ADVENT?

What's one memory from today that I will carry with me?

… THE GLORIOUS ONE

DAY TWENTY-FOUR

HAS COME

LUKE 2:21-40

THE CIRCUMCISION AND PRESENTATION OF JESUS

²¹ When the eight days were completed for his circumcision, he was named Jesus—the name given by the angel before he was conceived. ²² And when the days of their purification according to the law of Moses were finished, they brought him up to Jerusalem to present him to the Lord ²³ (just as it is written in the law of the Lord, Every firstborn male will be dedicated to the Lord) ²⁴ and to offer a sacrifice (according to what is stated in the law of the Lord, a pair of turtledoves or two young pigeons).

SIMEON'S PROPHETIC PRAISE

²⁵ There was a man in Jerusalem whose name was Simeon. This man was righteous and devout, looking forward to Israel's consolation, and the Holy Spirit was on him. ²⁶ It had been revealed to him by the Holy Spirit that he would not see death before he saw the Lord's Messiah. ²⁷ Guided by the Spirit, he entered the temple. When the parents brought in the child Jesus to perform for him what was customary under the law, ²⁸ Simeon took him up in his arms, praised God, and said,

> ²⁹ Now, Master,
> you can dismiss your servant in peace,
> as you promised.
> ³⁰ For my eyes have seen your salvation.
> ³¹ You have prepared it
> in the presence of all peoples—
> ³² a light for revelation to the Gentiles
> and glory to your people Israel.

³³ His father and mother were amazed at what was being said about him. ³⁴ Then Simeon blessed them and told his mother Mary, "Indeed, this child is destined to cause the fall and rise of many in Israel and to be a sign that will be opposed— ³⁵ and a sword will pierce your own soul—that the thoughts of many hearts may be revealed."

NOTES

ANNA'S TESTIMONY

[36] There was also a prophetess, Anna, a daughter of Phanuel, of the tribe of Asher. She was well along in years, having lived with her husband seven years after her marriage, [37] and was a widow for eighty-four years. She did not leave the temple, serving God night and day with fasting and prayers. [38] At that very moment, she came up and began to thank God and to speak about him to all who were looking forward to the redemption of Jerusalem.

THE FAMILY'S RETURN TO NAZARETH

[39] When they had completed everything according to the law of the Lord, they returned to Galilee, to their own town of Nazareth. [40] The boy grew up and became strong, filled with wisdom, and God's grace was on him.

ISAIAH 9:2

The people walking in darkness
have seen a great light;
a light has dawned
on those living in the land of darkness.

ISAIAH 49:6, 13

[6] …he says,
"It is not enough for you to be my servant
raising up the tribes of Jacob
and restoring the protected ones of Israel.

I WILL ALSO MAKE YOU A LIGHT FOR THE NATIONS, TO BE MY SALVATION TO THE ENDS OF THE EARTH."

…

[13] Shout for joy, you heavens!
Earth, rejoice!
Mountains break into joyful shouts!
For the Lord has comforted his people,
and will have compassion on his afflicted ones.

PAUSE

DATE / /

> Use this space to praise Jesus for His coming or to pray about any areas where you are still longing to see or experience Him as the glorious One.

& REFLECT

JOY TO THE WORLD! THE LORD IS COME

WORDS: Isaac Watts   MUSIC: George Frederick Handel

ARRANGEMENT: Lowell Mason

THE ETERNAL KING HAS COME

DAY 25

MATTHEW 2

WISE MEN VISIT THE KING

¹ After Jesus was born in Bethlehem of Judea in the days of King Herod, wise men from the east arrived in Jerusalem, ² saying, "Where is he who has been born king of the Jews? For we saw his star at its rising and have come to worship him."

³ When King Herod heard this, he was deeply disturbed, and all Jerusalem with him. ⁴ So he assembled all the chief priests and scribes of the people and asked them where the Messiah would be born.

⁵ "In Bethlehem of Judea," they told him, "because this is what was written by the prophet:

> ⁶ And you, Bethlehem, in the land of Judah,
> are by no means least among the rulers
>   of Judah:
> Because out of you will come a ruler
> who will shepherd my people Israel."

⁷ Then Herod secretly summoned the wise men and asked them the exact time the star appeared. ⁸ He sent them to Bethlehem and said, "Go and search carefully for the child. When you find him, report back to me so that I too can go and worship him."

⁹ After hearing the king, they went on their way. And there it was—the star they had seen at its rising. It led them until it came and stopped above the place where the child was. ¹⁰ When they saw the star, they were overwhelmed with joy. ¹¹ Entering the house, they saw the child with Mary his mother,

AND FALLING TO THEIR KNEES, THEY WORSHIPED HIM. THEN THEY OPENED THEIR TREASURES AND PRESENTED HIM WITH GIFTS: GOLD, FRANKINCENSE, AND MYRRH.

[12] And being warned in a dream not to go back to Herod, they returned to their own country by another route.

THE FLIGHT INTO EGYPT

[13] After they were gone, an angel of the Lord appeared to Joseph in a dream, saying, "Get up! Take the child and his mother, flee to Egypt, and stay there until I tell you. For Herod is about to search for the child to kill him." [14] So he got up, took the child and his mother during the night, and escaped to Egypt. [15] He stayed there until Herod's death, so that what was spoken by the Lord through the prophet might be fulfilled: Out of Egypt I called my Son.

THE MASSACRE OF THE INNOCENTS

[16] Then Herod, when he realized that he had been outwitted by the wise men, flew into a rage. He gave orders to massacre all the boys in and around Bethlehem who were two years old and under, in keeping with the time he had learned from the wise men. [17] Then what was spoken through Jeremiah the prophet was fulfilled:

[18] A voice was heard in Ramah,

> weeping, and great mourning,
> Rachel weeping for her children;
> and she refused to be consoled,
> because they are no more.

THE RETURN TO NAZARETH

[19] After Herod died, an angel of the Lord appeared in a dream to Joseph in Egypt, [20] saying, "Get up, take the child and his mother, and go to the land of Israel, because those who intended to kill the child are dead." [21] So he got up, took the child and his mother, and entered the land of Israel. [22] But when he heard that Archelaus was ruling over Judea in place of his father Herod, he was afraid to go there. And being warned in a dream, he withdrew to the region of Galilee.

NOTES

²³ Then he went and settled in a town called Nazareth to fulfill what was spoken through the prophets, that he would be called a Nazarene.

ISAIAH 60:1-3

THE LORD'S GLORY IN ZION

¹ Arise, shine, for your light has come,
and the glory of the LORD shines over you.
² For look, darkness will cover the earth,
and total darkness the peoples;
but the LORD will shine over you,
and his glory will appear over you.

**³ NATIONS WILL COME TO YOUR LIGHT,
AND KINGS TO YOUR SHINING BRIGHTNESS.**

PAUSE

DATE / /

Use this space to praise Jesus for His coming or to pray about any areas where you are still longing to see or experience Him as the eternal King.

& REFLECT

THE HOLY SPIRIT HAS COME

DAY 26

THE HOLY SPIRIT IS THE DOWN PAYMENT OF OUR INHERITANCE, UNTIL THE REDEMPTION OF THE POSSESSION, TO THE PRAISE OF HIS GLORY.

EPHESIANS 1:14

JOHN 20:30-31

³⁰ Jesus performed many other signs in the presence of his disciples that are not written in this book. ³¹ But these are written so that you may believe that Jesus is the Messiah, the Son of God, and that by believing you may have life in his name.

HEBREWS 1:1-3

THE NATURE OF THE SON

¹ Long ago God spoke to our ancestors by the prophets at different times and in different ways. ² In these last days, he has spoken to us by his Son. God has appointed him heir of all things and made the universe through him. ³ The Son is the radiance of God's glory and the exact expression of his nature, sustaining all things by his powerful word. After making purification for sins, he sat down at the right hand of the Majesty on high.

JOHN 14:18

"I will not leave you as orphans; I am coming to you."

JOHN 16:7-11

⁷ "Nevertheless, I am telling you the truth. It is for your benefit that I go away, because if I don't go away the Counselor will not come to you. If I go, I will send him to you. ⁸ When he comes, he will convict the world about sin, righteousness, and judgment: ⁹ About sin, because they do not believe in me; ¹⁰ about righteousness, because I am going to the Father and you will no longer see me; ¹¹ and about judgment, because the ruler of this world has been judged."

ACTS 2:1-4, 14-21

PENTECOST

¹ When the day of Pentecost had arrived, they were all together in one place. ² Suddenly a sound like that of a violent rushing wind came from heaven, and it filled the whole house where they were staying. ³ They saw tongues like flames of fire that separated and rested on each one of them. ⁴ Then they were all filled with the Holy Spirit and began to speak in different tongues, as the Spirit enabled them.

...

NOTES

PETER'S SERMON

[14] Peter stood up with the Eleven, raised his voice, and proclaimed to them, "Fellow Jews and all you residents of Jerusalem, let this be known to you, and pay attention to my words. [15] For these people are not drunk, as you suppose, since it's only nine in the morning. [16] On the contrary, this is what was spoken through the prophet Joel:

[17] And it will be in the last days, says God,
that I will pour out my Spirit on all people;
then your sons and your daughters will prophesy,
your young men will see visions,
and your old men will dream dreams.
[18] I will even pour out my Spirit
on my servants in those days, both men and women
and they will prophesy.
[19] I will display wonders in the heaven above
and signs on the earth below:
blood and fire and a cloud of smoke.
[20] The sun will be turned to darkness
and the moon to blood
before the great and glorious day of the Lord comes.
[21] Then everyone who calls
on the name of the Lord will be saved."

EPHESIANS 1:11-14

[11] In him we have also received an inheritance, because we were predestined according to the plan of the one who works out everything in agreement with the purpose of his will, [12] so that we who had already put our hope in Christ might bring praise to his glory.

[13] In him you also were sealed with the promised Holy Spirit when you heard the word of truth, the gospel of your salvation, and when you believed. [14] The Holy Spirit is the down payment of our inheritance, until the redemption of the possession, to the praise of his glory.

PAUSE

DATE / /

Use this space to rejoice in the coming of the Holy Spirit and to pray about any areas where you still long to experience what you've read about in Scripture.

& REFLECT

O COME, LET US ADORE HIM

WORDS: John F. Wade   MUSIC: Frederick Oakeley

HE ALONE IS WORTHY

THE EVERLASTING ONE WILL

WEEK 04

DAY 27

COME AGAIN

JOHN 14:2-3

² "In my Father's house are many rooms. If it were not so, would I have told you that I am going to prepare a place for you? ³ If I go away and prepare a place for you, I will come again and take you to myself, so that where I am you may be also."

ACTS 1:3-11

³ After he had suffered, he also presented himself alive to them by many convincing proofs, appearing to them over a period of forty days and speaking about the kingdom of God.

THE HOLY SPIRIT PROMISED

⁴ While he was with them, he commanded them not to leave Jerusalem, but to wait for the Father's promise. "Which," he said, "you have heard me speak about; ⁵ for John baptized with water, but you will be baptized with the Holy Spirit in a few days."

⁶ So when they had come together, they asked him, "Lord, are you restoring the kingdom to Israel at this time?"

⁷ He said to them, "It is not for you to know times or periods that the Father has set by his own authority. ⁸ But you will receive power when the Holy Spirit has come on you, and you will be my witnesses in Jerusalem, in all Judea and Samaria, and to the ends of the earth."

THE ASCENSION

⁹ After he had said this, he was taken up as they were watching, and a cloud took him out of their sight. ¹⁰ While he was going, they were gazing into heaven, and suddenly two men in white clothes stood by them. ¹¹ They said, "Men of Galilee, why do you stand looking up into heaven?

THIS SAME JESUS, WHO HAS BEEN TAKEN FROM YOU INTO HEAVEN, WILL COME IN THE SAME WAY THAT YOU HAVE SEEN HIM GOING INTO HEAVEN."

REVELATION 19:11–16

THE RIDER ON A WHITE HORSE

[11] Then I saw heaven opened, and there was a white horse. Its rider is called Faithful and True, and with justice he judges and makes war. [12] His eyes were like a fiery flame, and many crowns were on his head. He had a name written that no one knows except himself. [13] He wore a robe dipped in blood, and his name is called the Word of God. [14] The armies that were in heaven followed him on white horses, wearing pure white linen. [15] A sharp sword came from his mouth, so that he might strike the nations with it. He will rule them with an iron rod. He will also trample the winepress of the fierce anger of God, the Almighty. [16] And he has a name written on his robe and on his thigh: King of Kings and Lord of Lords.

REVELATION 22:20

He who testifies about these things says, "Yes, I am coming soon."

Amen! Come, Lord Jesus!

PAUSE

DATE / /

Use this space to praise Jesus for His coming or to pray about any areas where you are still longing to see or experience Him as the everlasting One who will come again.

DAY 28 — GRACE

DAY

DAY

GRACE

DAY 28

Take this day to catch up on your reading, pray, and rest in the presence of the Lord.

Long ago God spoke to our ancestors by the prophets at different times and in different ways. In these last days, he has spoken to us by his Son. God has appointed him heir of all things and made the universe through him.

Hebrews 1:1–2

THE LAST SUNDAY OF THE YEAR

> "AND REMEMBER, I AM WITH YOU ALWAYS, TO THE END OF THE AGE."
>
> MATTHEW 28:20

For this last day of 2023, use the following pages to reflect on what Advent has meant to you this season and to remember your time in the Word this year.

Thanks be to God that He is indeed with us always, in our deepest longings for His presence and our hope for Him to come again.

FOR THE
RECORD

My favorite passage from this Advent study:

_____
_____
_____
_____
_____
_____

MY FAVORITE DAY IN THIS ADVENT STUDY:

1	2	3	4	5	6
7	8	9	10	11	12
13	14	15	16	17	18
19	20	21	22	23	24
25	26	27	28	29	

How did my time in Scripture this Advent strengthen my understanding of who Jesus is?

_____
_____
_____
_____
_____
_____
_____
_____

What will it look like for me to remember and trust in Jesus beyond this Advent season?

_____
_____
_____
_____
_____
_____
_____
_____

What did I learn this Advent that I want to share with someone else?

IN 2023...

How did I see God at work over the past year?

_____
_____
_____
_____
_____
_____
_____

SOMETHING GOD TAUGHT ME ABOUT HIS CHARACTER:

SOMETHING GOD TAUGHT ME ABOUT MYSELF:

SOMETHING GOD IS GROWING IN ME:

An unexpected surprise:

An unexpected sorrow:

I'm most proud of:

The highlight of my year:

MY PRAYER FOR

2024

DON'T STOP READING NOW—START YOUR YEAR IN SCRIPTURE!
Join us for our new study, *Everything New,* beginning Monday, January 1.

Tips for Memorizing Scripture

At He Reads Truth, we believe Scripture memorization is an important discipline in your walk with God. Committing God's Truth to memory means He can minister to us—and we can minister to others—through His Word no matter where we are. As you approach the Weekly Truth passage in this book, try these memorization tips to see which techniques work best for you.

STUDY IT

Study the passage in its biblical context and ask yourself a few questions before you begin to memorize it: What does this passage say? What does it mean? How would I say this in my own words? What does it teach me about God? Understanding what the passage means helps you know why it is important to carry it with you wherever you go.

Break the passage into smaller sections, memorizing a phrase at a time.

PRAY IT

Use the passage you are memorizing as a prompt for prayer.

WRITE IT

Dedicate a notebook to Scripture memorization and write the passage over and over again.

Diagram the passage after you write it out. Place a square around the verbs, underline the nouns, and circle any adjectives or adverbs. Say the passage aloud several times, emphasizing the verbs as you repeat it. Then do the same thing again with the nouns, then the adjectives and adverbs.

Write out the first letter of each word in the passage somewhere you can reference it throughout the week as you work on your memorization.

Use a whiteboard to write out the passage. Erase a few words at a time as you continue to repeat it aloud. Keep erasing parts of the passage until you have it all committed to memory.

CREATE

If you can, make up a tune for the passage to sing as you go about your day, or try singing it to the tune of a favorite song.

Use hand signals or signs to come up with associations for each word or phrase and repeat the movements as you practice.

SAY IT

Repeat the passage out loud to yourself as you are going through the rhythm of your day—getting ready, pouring your coffee, waiting in traffic, or making dinner.

Listen to the passage read aloud to you.

Record a voice memo on your phone and listen to it throughout the day or play it on an audio Bible.

SHARE IT

Memorize the passage with a friend, family member, or mentor. Spontaneously challenge each other to recite the passage, or pick a time to review your passage and practice saying it from memory together.

Send the passage as an encouraging text to a friend, testing yourself as you type to see how much you have memorized so far.

KEEP AT IT

Set reminders on your phone to prompt you to practice your passage.

Keep a stack of note cards with Scripture you are memorizing by your bed. Practice reciting what you've memorized previously before you go to sleep, ending with the passages you are currently learning. If you wake up in the middle of the night, review them again instead of grabbing your phone. Read them out loud before you get out of bed in the morning.

CSB BOOK ABBREVIATIONS

OLD TESTAMENT

GN Genesis	**JB** Job	**HAB** Habakkuk	**PHP** Philippians
EX Exodus	**PS** Psalms	**ZPH** Zephaniah	**COL** Colossians
LV Leviticus	**PR** Proverbs	**HG** Haggai	**1TH** 1 Thessalonians
NM Numbers	**EC** Ecclesiastes	**ZCH** Zechariah	**2TH** 2 Thessalonians
DT Deuteronomy	**SG** Song of Solomon	**MAL** Malachi	**1TM** 1 Timothy
JOS Joshua	**IS** Isaiah		**2TM** 2 Timothy
JDG Judges	**JR** Jeremiah	### NEW TESTAMENT	**TI** Titus
RU Ruth	**LM** Lamentations	**MT** Matthew	**PHM** Philemon
1SM 1 Samuel	**EZK** Ezekiel	**MK** Mark	**HEB** Hebrews
2SM 2 Samuel	**DN** Daniel	**LK** Luke	**JMS** James
1KG 1 Kings	**HS** Hosea	**JN** John	**1PT** 1 Peter
2KG 2 Kings	**JL** Joel	**AC** Acts	**2PT** 2 Peter
1CH 1 Chronicles	**AM** Amos	**RM** Romans	**1JN** 1 John
2CH 2 Chronicles	**OB** Obadiah	**1CO** 1 Corinthians	**2JN** 2 John
EZR Ezra	**JNH** Jonah	**2CO** 2 Corinthians	**3JN** 3 John
NEH Nehemiah	**MC** Micah	**GL** Galatians	**JD** Jude
EST Esther	**NAH** Nahum	**EPH** Ephesians	**RV** Revelation

BIBLIOGRAPHY Gross, Bobby. *Living the Christian Year: Time to Inhabit the Story of God.* Downers Grove: InterVarsity Press, 2012.

HE READS TRUTH	ROMANS
HE READS TRUTH	THE GENEALOGY OF JESUS
HE READS TRUTH	AMOS
HE READS TRUTH	A LIVING HOPE: A BIBLICAL STUDY OF RESURRECTED LIFE IN CHRIST
HE READS TRUTH	LENT 2023
HE READS TRUTH	I WILL GIVE YOU REST: AN INVITATION TO SABBATH
HE READS TRUTH	THE LIFE OF JESUS: AS RECORDED BY MATTHEW, MARK, AND LUKE

SIGN UP FOR THE
SUBSCRIPTION BOX AT
HEREADSTRUTH.COM/SUBBOX

JOIN OUR TEXT CLUB AND
GET 20% OFF YOUR NEXT ORDER!

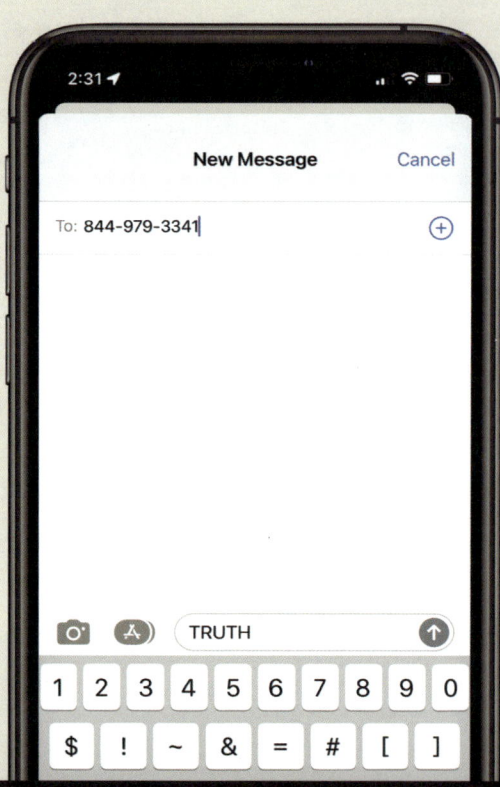

JUST TEXT "**TRUTH**" TO 844-979-3341

Have questions? Email us at **HELLO@SHEREADSTRUTH.COM**

By signing up via text, you agree to receive recurring automated promotional and personalized marketing text messages (e.g. cart reminders) from She Reads Truth at the cell number used when signing up. Consent is not a condition of any purchase. Reply HELP for help and STOP to cancel. Msg frequency varies. Msg & data rates may apply. View Terms & Privacy. Offer is limited to inventory on hand and excludes monthly/annual subscriptions, Bibles, and gift cards.